vietnam war literature

An annotated bibliography of
imaginative works about
Americans fighting in Vietnam

by JOHN NEWMAN

THE SCARECROW PRESS, INC.
Metuchen, N.J., & London • 1982

Library of Congress Cataloging in Publication Data

Newman, John, 1942–
    Vietnam War literature.

    Includes index.
    1. American literature--20th century--Bibliography.
2. Vietnamese Conflict, 1961-1975, in literature--
Bibliography. 3. War in literature--Bibliography.
I. Title.
Z1227.N49 [PS228.V5] 016.81'08'0358   81-21509
ISBN 0-8108-1514-1   AACR2

DEDICATION

This book is dedicated to the Americans
who fought their country's war in Vietnam.

ACKNOWLEDGMENTS

This bibliography could not have been compiled without much assistance from friends and colleagues at Colorado State University Libraries. Research and writing was done during a sabbatical leave granted for that purpose by the governing board of Colorado State University. Special thanks for active help are due to Donna Leflar, John Clark Pratt, and Pat Egan.

TABLE OF CONTENTS

FOREWORD

John Clark Pratt

Vietnam/Thailand/Laos   August 1969 - August 1970

For a Vietnam veteran, to read through John Newman's bibliography is to relive the war. As are the literary works
themselves, the significant events, sights, and feelings are
documented here: the trauma, the internal conflicts, the
atrocities, the heroism, the misunderstandings, the loves,
the losses, and yes, even the humor. John has combined
sincere scholarship with unusually dispassionate insight, and
this first annotated guide to Vietnam fiction and poetry is not
only a significant contribution to literary history but also an
important documentation of the breadth of writing done about
America's longest war.

In 1975, when John and I first discussed the possibil-
ities of such a collection, we knew of about fifty novels,
quite a few poems, and some short stories. One has only
to look at the publication dates noted in this bibliography to
realize how ignorant we, along with so many other Americans,
were. An incident that occurred soon afterward is an example: for a 1976 talk I was preparing on Vietnam War literature, I queried major U. S. publishers about their offerings.
One leading editor-in-chief replied that his firm had published
no Vietnam War fiction; nor did he intend to, because it
would not sell. Subsequent investigation showed that his company had already published three novels about the war. It is
as if this editor had done what so many other Americans have
done: simply block out the facts of this most unpopular war.

Thanks to John Newman, as well as a few others who
have been working quietly to preserve what the Vietnam War
really was, those authors who wrote about the war can now

have their voices heard. Readers can now start with the
annotations in Newman's work. His summary comments, re-
sulting from months of immersion in the literature, indicate
mainly what the work is about, and, as an annotated bibliography should do, abstain remarkably from editorial bias (ex-
cept in a few instances where the work in question is unmiti-
gated trash whose relevance to Vietnam is purely exploitative).
Knowing John Newman as I do, I had expected far more sub-
jective analyses. I was wrong, and I would suggest that future readers for whom this bibliography will provide a necessary starting point profitably emulate the careful, sincere
attention to objectivity. Perhaps for the first time since the
outbreak of hostilities (whenever that really was), an analysis
of Vietnam-related material has been made without overween-
ing bias.

This bibliography accordingly stands as a work of
scholarship to which all that follow will be mere revisions
and addenda. Certainly, there have been omissions, particularly in regard to poetry, where many of the original fugitive
pieces were never cataloged. Information about and especially
copies of any missing literary publications would be welcomed,
because the Vietnam War Literature Collection at Colorado
State University is an ongoing project.

Finally, I would like to echo John Newman's dedica-
tion of this work to those who served. Now, years after the
official ending of hostilities, only by reading about the way
it seemed to those who wrote about it can Americans perhaps finally understand how the Vietnam War really was.

J. C. P.
12 January 1982

PREFACE

Background

This annotated bibliography is based primarily upon materials in the Vietnam War Literature Collection at Colorado State University in Fort Collins. That collection was begun in 1975 after a nationwide survey of large research libraries revealed that not one of them was collecting the fiction, poetry, and other creative works about the American military effort in Vietnam. In the past six years, the CSU collection has come to be known to those who write and study Vietnam War literature as a unique and complete resource. The informed good will of interested writers, scholars, and booksellers is essential for any special book collection, especially for a new one such as this, which seeks material that is often both elusive and obscure.

This book is intended as a guide to the literature for scholars, students, and others who may be interested in it. Another purpose is to inform those same persons about the CSU collection in the hope that some of them will provide information that will enhance its growth and potential for service.

Scope

This bibliography lists novels, short stories, poetry collections, such miscellaneous works as humor and cartoon collections, and drama published through early 1981. Nonfiction and books of photographs are omitted. Some diaries, personal narratives, and so-called "new journalism" or "nonfiction novels" have much to say about the Vietnam experience, and many are quite similar in appearance to novels, but there are enough pure novels from which

to choose, and it seemed unwise to blur definitions in this
study.

The scope of this bibliography also excludes novels
about the French in Indochina and about politicians and dip-
lomats in Vietnam or Vietnam-like countries prior to participation of Americans in the actual war. It does, however,
include works set in Laos and Cambodia, and some books
are cited here that describe fighting in imaginary countries
that clearly represent Vietnam.

The returning Vietnam serviceman and the Vietnam
veteran occur as characters in a number of books. The
practice here is to accept such works if the Vietnam experience is actually described or if the war experience is essential to the characters' thoughts and actions.

The essential criterion for works cited here is that
they depict Americans fighting in Vietnam. This excludes
much of the protest literature that appeared in great volume
in the 1960s and 1970s; these works often refer to Vietnam,
but few are set there. It should be pointed out that many
of the titles in this bibliography, written by embittered veterans, have a strong and clear antiwar message.

Major bibliographic tools, among them the Library of
Congress subject catalogs and the Short Story Index, take a
broader view of Vietnam War literature. In some instances,
they list books and stories that are written in the context of
the Vietnam War but that may contain only passing reference
to it. The present compiler's narrower definition emerged
from his concern to present works that describe the Vietnam
War as it was seen firsthand by those who fought it and on
television by those who did not.

Even within this limited range, it has not been possible to see everything. An appendix lists titles that are
confidently believed to be appropriate for this bibliography
but that could not be located in time to meet the publication
deadline.

Entries

The standard bibliographic entries used here should be familiar to most persons. Publishers' names are given in full,

as they appear on title pages. This may not be absolutely
necessary for well-known trade, subsidy, and academic publishers, but it is intended to be informative and helpful in
the many instances of those that are virtually unknown, especially those that may have existed only to put out a single
title.

Pagination is given in order to convey an idea of a
work's size and also to provide precise information for readers who may wish to order copies of material from periodicals through interlibrary loan.

Library of Congress numbers are supplied whenever
they are known. Even large libraries are no longer self-
sufficient; cooperative networks and interlibrary loan are facts
of modern scholarly life. Library of Congress numbers are
useful descriptors for entry into the electronic bibliographic
utilities that connect many large research libraries to one
another.

Although the first goal of this bibliography is to iden-
tify as many titles as possible, the indication of variant edi-
tions is an important secondary objective. As many are in-
cluded in the entries as could be found.

Each format has its own problems and opportunities
for citations. Monographs, especially novels from trade publishers, are usually quite easy because their bibliographic
details appear on the preliminary pages and elsewhere in a
standardized and accurate manner. Short stories, on the
other hand, are often confusingly complex, and some effort
is required to see that the entries for them are not. Many
short stories are reprinted in collections, and others change
in both title and substance. This literary richness produces
a plethora of bibliographic detail, but the entries are laid out
in the most routine and complete manner that could be de-
vised.

Annotations

The compiler has read every work noted here, and from the
annotations a judgment can be made whether they were all
understood. In description of books whose components are so
very similar to one another, some monotony is inevitable, but
the compiler has attempted to look at each item as a unique

literary effort, separate from others and separate, for the
most part, from the actual history of the Vietnam War.
These works are imaginative; it would be unfair and limiting
to evaluate them as history. There is no shortage of historical and other nonfiction books about the Vietnam War.

Although works vary in the details of the information
they convey, the annotations seek generally to relate certain
essentials about each title. These include the dates of the
story, the location (whether real or notional) in Vietnam, the
rank and duties of the characters, the plot, and sometimes
the compiler's opinion of the work's literary or other qualities.
In this last regard, it is worth mentioning that the compiler
is a librarian writing annotations, not a critic or a professional student of modern literature writing reviews.

The annotations for poetry are brief and they usually
describe only the externals of the works listed. Criticism
of poetry is better left to those with appropriate experience
and training.

This bibliography will have served its purpose if it provides
the basis for further study of the literature of America's
most recent and unsettling war.

VIETNAM WAR LITERATURE

BIBLIOGRAPHY AND SCHOLARSHIP

Vietnam War literature has given birth to a large body of secondary work. In addition to the studies selected for this brief discussion, there are numerous general articles and even more reviews of individual titles. Some attempt is being made at Colorado State University to collect pertinent secondary material, and in the future, the files on hand may provide the basis for a published bibliography.

Those who study Vietnam War literature are fortunate in that Peter Leonard Stromberg provides so much useful information and sets such a fine example of bibliography and criticism in his 1974 Ph. D. dissertation at Cornell University, The Long War's Writing: American Novels About the Fighting in Vietnam Written While Americans Fought. Stromberg is a professional Army officer with service in Vietnam, and he brings that perspective, as well as the training of a scholar, to this penetrating criticism of all important novels within his period. His dissertation lacks an index, which would be useful, but an itemized table of contents and a fine bibliography serve well.

Similar in scope to Leonard, but naturally much shorter, is Wayne Miller's "Southeast Asia; the War in Fiction," a paper read at the 1972 Modern Language Association meeting in New York. To Miller's thoughtful paper belongs the distinction of being one of the first scholarly studies of Vietnam fiction.

The largest published enumerative bibliography, compiled by Tom Colonnese and Jerry Hogan, appears as "Vietnam War Literature, 1958-1979; A First Checklist," in Bulletin of Bibliography for January-March 1981. The compilers worked from other bibliographies, including a preliminary checklist provided to them from the CSU collection, and there-

3

fore were not able to see all the material they cite. Bibliographic details and accuracy vary considerably, and the assignment of some items to categories is questionable, but
the value of this checklist is its comprehensiveness, especially as it includes some nonfiction, "new journalism," and
criticism.

Novels are arranged in chronological and subject categories, associated with nonfiction works, in The Vietnam
Era; A Guide to Teaching Resources (Indochina Curriculum
Group, 1978). This guide is prepared for high school teach-
ers, but it will serve more advanced students as well. The
arrangement is logical, bibliographic details are complete
and correct, and the annotations are thorough.

Some general studies have now begun to touch on
Vietnam literature. In his War and the Novelist (University
of Missouri Press, 1976), Peter Jones discusses several
Vietnam novels in the larger context of all war fiction.
Myron R. Smith, Jr.'s War Story Guide (Scarecrow Press,
1981) lists 3,917 briefly annotated entries, seventy of which
are Vietnam titles.

It is to support research and scholarship that the
Vietnam War Literature Collection exists. Several studies
are under way at present, and scholars working on this topic
are invited to write to the compiler to explore matters of
mutual interest.

NOVELS

1. Anderson, William C. The Gooney Bird. New York:
    Crown Publishers, Inc., 1968. 306pp. 68-
    20458.

    The use of an antiquated, slow-flying, transport plane
    as a platform for machine guns is tactically fascinat-
    ing. In addition to describing that innovation, this
    book offers a certain look at the attitudes and prac-
    tices of military pilots. Unfortunately, the characters
    are rather shallow and quite similar to one another.
    If this book is to be believed, the air war in Vietnam
    was fought by enthusiastic, wisecracking officers,
    every one of whom was a memorable personality.
    The wounded and dying are heroic and quiet, and the
    survivors return home with minor wounds and much
    glory. The pilots are essentially indifferent to the
    ground beneath them. The story happens to be set
    in Vietnam, but there is little background description
    and no significant Vietnamese characters appear.

2. Atkinson, Hugh. The Most Savage Animal. London:
    Rupert Hart-Davis, 1972. 373pp. 71-139615.
    New York: Simon and Schuster, nd.

    An unusual and interesting international perspective on
    the Vietnam War emerges in this novel of the Interna-
    tional Committee of the Red Cross. It is set both in
    Europe and in Vietnam around 1969, and the numerous
    characters include executives, doctors, and volunteers
    for the Red Cross, as well as Americans and Viet-
    namese fighting the war. The plot has two main
    threads. One is an attempt by International Red Cross
    officials to politicize the organization in an anti-

American fashion and the other is a scheme to smuggle
plague-infested rats into the United States aboard trans-
port aircraft.   There are numerous subplots.   Several
battle scenes are chilling and convincing, but the book
seems to have no central focus as a story.   It does
provide, however, a view of the humanitarian effort
in Vietnam and of European manners and attitudes
that are not often found in books about this war.

3.   Baber, Asa.   The Land of a Million Elephants.   New
         York;   William Morrow and Company, Inc.,
         1970.   152pp.   71-103886.

In contrast to real life, this tale of the mythical king-
dom of Chanda describes its people in their successful attempt to resist importation of the general Southeast Asian war.   Chanda can be reached by air from
Saigon, and it is clearly an artificial analog to Laos.
The country is host to military advisers, diplo-
mats, and spies from major European and Asian na-
tions.   After these individuals manage to introduce
the beginnings of a war, the inhabitants of Chanda
flee to the Plain of Elephants, where their folk magic
protects them from both Russian tanks and American
atomic bombs.   In this story of what might have been,
the peaceful life endures.   The style, which is similar
to that of a folk story or children's tale, enhances literary quality and sustained humor without becoming
wearing or tedious.   This is a sophisticated and successful piece of writing.

4.   Baker, Richard E.   Feast of Epiphany.   Tacoma,
         Washington: The Rapier Press, 1981.   186pp.
         80-85403.

The dust wrapper offers the information that this book
should be "learned not understood."   That is no doubt
good advice, because a single careful reading produces
little or no understanding of the author's plot or purposes.   The characters are enlisted men in the 4th
Infantry Division band who serve as infantry around
Pleiku in what seems to be 1966.   There is no sense
of the general tactical situation, and the men function
more as a loose gang than as members of an organized

military unit. There are occasions of crucifixion and
homosexuality, as well as a bit of combat and a lengthy
report of a leave in Hong Kong. Difficulty in follow-
ing the book is exacerbated by spelling and grammat-
ical errors and by extremely poor reproduction. Baker
clearly has something to say about the war, but he
does not say it clearly. The book would have been
much improved by better editing.

5.   Barfield, H. Eugene. Treachery on the Double.
      Hicksville, New York: Exposition Press, 1979.
      150pp.

The literary quality of many Vietnam War novels is
not particularly high, but this one is almost painful
to read. Short chapters, a choppy text, superficial
characters, and implausible dialogue combine to con-
fuse and bore the reader. Set mostly in Thailand,
the plot has to do with an attempt by Air Force officers and NCOs to stop a drug-smuggling operation
conducted by Chinese and Albanians. Among many
low points is a lengthy explanation of the supposed effects of marijuana that might have been given in a
grade-school classroom sometime in the 1950s. The
author is clearly a patriotic man who can describe
Asian and military scenes with some accuracy, but
this story has neither credibility nor cohesion.

6.   Biersach, Frank J., Jr. So Cruel World. np: np,
      1968.

The paper, typeface, and method of construction suggest that this book may have been manufactured in
Asia. Reproduction is especially bad. Many letters
are illegible, and some corrections appear to have
been made in the review copy with a typewriter. The
story has to do with the younger members of a Vietnamese family and their association with an American
officer in Saigon in 1965. One of the sons of the family becomes an independent newspaper editor; the other
is a Vietcong terrorist who is sent to kill him. The
narration and dialogue are stilted and awkward, and
there is much pontification about the causes, rights,
and wrongs of the Vietnam War. This book must have

been produced privately, and it clearly has not been
edited in any customary manner.

7.   Blacker, Irwin P. Search and Destroy. New York:
        Random House, 1966. 274 pp. 66-21492.

The title is a bit misleading, for this is an account
of a commando-type raid into North Vietnam. After
learning of the construction of an airfield, a dam,
and fuel storage facilities near Hanoi, an American
President determines that bombing them would run too
great a risk of war with Russia and China. Instead,
he sends in a small group of men on the ground.
Their background and training are recounted completely,
but details about military procedures and weapons are
not always accurate. At one point, a general commanding a secret national military agency flies into
North Vietnam to assist. The team completes its
mission and destroys the facilities, but nearly all of
its members are killed. The Vietnamese appear hardly
at all in this story; it is essentially a military adventure.

8.   Boatman, Alan. Comrades in Arms. New York:
        Harper & Row, Publishers, 1974. 229pp.
        74-4139.

Boatman is an able novelist. His characters are
subtle and believable, and their thoughts, words, and
actions are interesting. In the first part of the book,
a Marine corporal, Harding, is shot in the back by a
black Marine. The motive could be attempted murder
or simple incompetence; the reasons are vague. In
any case, Harding's friends later murder the assailant.
Harding is evacuated from Vietnam, and he awaits
medical discharge at Marine bases in California and
North Carolina. Like many of his friends, Harding
is a draftee who chose the Marine Corps instead of
flight from the war. Conversations among these
characters are revealing. Among his other literary
talents, Boatman is well able to evoke the sleazy at-
mosphere of military camp towns, with their bars,
whores, and streets.

9.   Bosse, M. J. The Incident at Naha. New York:

Simon and Schuster, 1972. 221pp. 72-179588.
London: Macmillan, 1972.

The narrator is a young white woman, living in New York with her black lover, Virgil. He is a man of unbelievable beauty, strength, courage, intellect, integrity, and philosophical depth. Virgil had served as a lieutenant in a unit that had been remotely involved in a massacre of civilians in Vietnam. When another former member of the unit is murdered, Virgil and his lady begin a search through the man's papers. These, reproduced at great length in the text, have to do with Commodore Perry's mission to Japan. The murder is finally solved, and the Vietnam connection is one of many historical threads drawn together to achieve a solution.

10. Briley, John. The Traitors. New York: G. P. Putnam's Sons, 1969. 441pp. 78-81568.

The subject of treachery is handled well and at considerable length in this novel by an American living in England. A squad of American soldiers is captured in South Vietnam, probably sometime in the late 1960s. They are taken to North Vietnam, where some of them are persuaded by a defector, Evans, to assist with a mission to rescue an important communist from a South Vietnamese military jail. The characters, including some Vietnamese, have complete and complex personalities, and their conversations are interesting and plausible. Indeed, much of the book is given over to talk about the rights and wrongs of the parties participating in the Vietnam War. The lives and military methods of the North Vietnamese appear in very great detail. The rescue mission and ensuing fight provide a climax in which many of the major characters are killed.

11. Brooke, Dinah. Games of Love and War. London: Jonathan Cape, 1976. 190pp.

Like its title, this book is almost a game. After the withdrawal of American troops and before the victory of communist forces in Vietnam, there was a confused

and ambivalent period. Into this environment come
Elspeth, a spoiled European girl, her businessman
father, and his mistress. Descriptions of Saigon,
Udorn, and other Southeast Asian locations, made
from a European point of view, constitute the best
parts of the book. American and Asian characters
are minor stereotypes, and the plot seems as pointless as the luxurious lives of the main characters.
The difficulty in understanding the action is increased
by frequent changes between first- and third-person
narration and by the use of the present tense for past,
present, and imagined action. Also, quotation marks
are absent.

12.   Brossard, Chandler. Wake Up. We're Almost There.
       New York: Richard W. Baron, 1971. 540pp.
       76-125552.

       With some effort, it is possible to locate three sec-
       tions of this large and complex novel that are set in
       Vietnam. In the two shorter passages, Cedric, a
       black homosexual, serves as a typical infantryman,
       involved in an ambush in the Central Highlands and
       in the subsequent occupation of a village. In the third
       and largest section, Bosworth Horn, a lieutenant of
       Cherokee Indian background, joins the Vietcong to
       bomb two American installations in Saigon. It is in
       no way clear how these incidents relate to each other
       or to the remainder of the book, whose plot seems
       to transcend time, space, and reality. Brossard is
       a noted and experienced novelist, but in this work the
       Vietnam sections are physically and contextually lost.

13.   Broun, Anthony. War and the Man-Lovers. np:
       Master Classic, nd. 160pp.

       The Vietnam War provides a perfunctory setting for
       this explicit homosexual novel, but there is no real
       attempt at background accuracy. The weapons, mil-
       itary slang, and tactics suggest that the author may
       have a sketchy knowledge of World War II or the
       Korean War.

14.   Browne, Corrine. Body Shop. New York: Stein

and Day/Publishers, 1973. 180pp. 73-
79226.

Most of the characters in this sensitive novel are
patients in the amputation ward of San Francisco
Army Hospital. The time is between 1970 and 1972,
and there are numerous, lengthy flashbacks that describe how several of the amputees grew up, joined
the military, fought in Vietnam, and were wounded.
The stories are often poignant, and the men respond
thoughtfully to the loss of one or more limbs. In
the hospital, they smoke dope frequently, enjoy good
relationships with one another and with the staff, and
seem self-aware. A few have given up hope entirely,
but the novel focuses on one man, Woody, who makes
a good and aggressive adjustment to civilian life.
With all its sensitivity and apparent veracity, the
book suffers from occasional proofreading errors, and
it would seem that the author is not completely familiar with initialisms and military terms.

15. Bunting, Josiah. The Lionheads. New York: George
Braziller, 1972. 213pp. 78-188356. New York:
Popular Library, nd.

There is often a considerable distance between the
views of generals who plan battles and the lower-
ranking men who must fight them. Bunting's touching
and cynical story, set in the Mekong Delta in March
of 1968, has to do with an attempt by an American
brigade to destroy a North Vietnamese main-force
battalion. Most of the characters are officers, including a careerist general who fights a battle to advance his own prospects. The general is successful,
but the battle is terribly costly to American forces.
Bunting describes the Mekong Delta with accuracy and
detail, and he clearly explains the problems of Americans fighting there, especially the high reliance upon
complicated equipment that does not always work.
There is no real attempt to personalize the enemy or
to describe his tactics, although he is perceived by
all the characters as being much more able than they
to operate in the difficult terrain of jungle and swamp.

16. Butterworth, W. E. Air Evac. New York: W. W.

Norton & Company, Inc. , 1967. 211pp. 67-
18675.

The first and largest portion of this novel describes
the family, social relationships, college career, and
ideas of a young man named Ken Maddox. It is set
in the mid-1960s, and Maddox must face the draft after college. As a near pacifist, he is unwilling to
kill, but he manages to be assigned to training as a
medical helicopter pilot in Alabama. In the last pages
of the book, Maddox goes to Vietnam, where he firms
up his personality and ideas. The reader is left with
the impression that Maddox may become a competent
professional officer. This novel is almost a juvenile.
The characters seldom drink, curse, or fornicate.
Their motives and ideas are always completely clear
(and simple). There is a wealth of information about
helicopters and military training, but little about Vietnam.

17. Butterworth, W. E. Orders to Vietnam. Boston:
        Little, Brown and Company, 1968. 145pp. 68-
        15387.

Like Butterworth's earlier Air Evac, this is a paean
to the Army in general and to helicopter pilots in particular. Bill Byers, the son of an Army general and
a dropout from West Point, is trained as a helicopter
pilot after being drafted. Byers is sent to Pleiku,
where he flies both unarmed craft and gunships in
numerous actions. The enemy hardly appear as characters; they are just targets on the ground. Vietnam
and the South Vietnamese also have little to do with
the story. Aircraft and their battles are described
in exhaustive detail. To his credit, Butterworth tries
to convey the spirit and military attitude of professional officers, but he is rather heavyhanded in the
attempt.

18. Cassidy, John. A Station in the Delta. New York:
        Charles Scribner's Sons, 1979. 380pp. 79-
        9819. New York: Ballantine Books, 1981.

The role of the Central Intelligence Agency was one

of many controversial aspects of the Vietnam War.
A Station in the Delta, written by a former CIA em-
ployee, provides an interesting look at how Agency
operations were, or may have been, conducted in
Vietnam. Toby Busch, an experienced agent, takes
over a station in the Mekong Delta and acquires intelligence that enables him to predict the 1968 Tet
offensive. However, Busch is unable to move his
information up through channels because of personal
and political problems within the Agency. These dif-
ficulties occupy much of the book, but in the end
Busch emerges as both professionally and personally
heroic. Cassidy makes the point that the Tet offensive was a military failure for the communists but
that it became a political victory because of misinter-
pretation by the U.S. news media and by civilians at
home.

19.   Chandler, David. Captain Hollister. New York:
      The Macmillan Company, 1973. 207pp. 72-
      90548.

Ernest Hollister, a Vietnam veteran and college professor, rejoins the Army and returns to Vietnam after
a six-year absence. The time seems to be around
1970. Hollister is assigned to a graves-registration
unit and finds himself writing letters of condolence to
survivors of dead men. Driven by motives that are
not completely clear, Hollister begins to write letters
describing the true circumstances of deaths. After a
brief experience in the field, Hollister joins with a
group of enlisted men to ship heroin back to the United
States in the bodies of dead servicemen. There is
some intimation that the heroin will somehow be used
to destabilize American society, but Hollister is killed
before he can see the plan through. Chandler is an
able novelist, but his point here is not quite under-
standable.

20.   Clark, Alan. The Lion Heart. New York: William
      Morrow and Company, 1969. 255pp. 69-11569.

Clark, an English military historian, writes with im-
pressive familiarity and accuracy about Americans.

His story is set in Central Vietnam, near the Cambodian border, in 1967. Jack Lane, a Special Forces
officer, is assigned to advise the newly arrived American 78th Division. Against Lane's advice, the general
commanding the division launches a classic military
operation, which ends in disaster. Lane is killed, but
the general manages to preserve his command and his
reputation with consummate political skill. All the
characters of any consequence are officers. While
the book ends on a neutral note insofar as the future
of the war is concerned, there is a good deal of emphasis on the corruption of the South Vietnamese and
the commitment of the Vietcong. Clark provides a
list of characters, a glossary of Vietnamese and military terms, and frequent explanatory footnotes.

21.   Coleman, Charles. Sergeant Back Again. New York:
          Harper & Row Publishers, 1980. 137pp. 80-
          7601.

This intense and serious novel tries too hard to make
its point. The patients at a military hospital in Texas
in 1970 must face the prospect of rehabilitation or
permanent transfer to a mental hospital. Each re-
lives his Vietnam experiences. One, Andrew Collins,
had served as a surgical technician and mutilated
himself to get out of the war. Collins had also been
involved with an underground GI antiwar organization.
Among the patients who are quite self-conscious about
their mental problems, Collins stands out. He admin-
isters a sort of self-therapy during an illegal leave,
but the ending, like the rest of the book, is confused
and lacking in balance.

22.   Collingwood, Charles. The Defector. New York:
          Harper & Row, Publishers, 1970. 313pp.
          77-103133. New York: Ace, nd.

Not surprisingly, the hero of this novel is a television
correspondent. During the Paris peace negotiations,
Bill Benson is recruited by the Central Intelligence
Agency to assist with the escape of a North Vietnamese government official who wishes to defect. The
descriptions of Hanoi, based on the author's visit there

in 1968, are fascinating, as are observations throughout about the toughness and commitment of the North
Vietnamese people. The defector is eventually es-
corted south to the Demilitarized Zone by Benson,
and the escape is made in a hail of gunfire. Once
inside South Vietnam, the escapee is murdered, and
the explanation emerges as a story of plots within
plots. Collingwood essentially ignores the ethical
issues that might be expected to confront a journalist
working for the CIA.

23.   Corder, E. M. The Deer Hunter. New York: Exeter
        Books, 1978. 189pp. 79-53098. New York:
        Jove Publications, Inc. , 1979.

Taken from the well-known motion picture of the same
name, The Deer Hunter describes the lives of a group
of young steelworkers from Pennsylvania who go to
war in Vietnam and suffer capture, mutilation, and
death. The motion picture is more a statement about
the war than an accurate depiction of it, and the book
follows the picture completely with a style that reveals
its origin: "She knocked. There was no answer. She
opened the door...." The value of this book is principally its accurate association with the motion picture,
which is thought by many to be a significant and tal-
ented reaction to the war.

24.   Crowther, John. Firebase. New York: St. Martin's
        Press, 1975. 207pp. 75-9489. London: Con-
        stable, 1975.

Military combat and the enemy barely appear in this
account of racial tension and violence at a remote
Army firebase. Instead of fighting the communists,
the black and white Americans kill one another. The
hero, Lt. Mather, works out the conflict between his
loyalties to the Army and to his fellow blacks as he
attempts to mitigate the actions of a racist commanding officer. The problems with this novel include
mistakes about military details and a rather florid
style, but the exploration of racial matters is interesting.

25.   Crumley, James. One to Count Cadence. New York:
       Random House, 1969. 338pp. 68-14518.

The U. S. Army before Vietnam was certainly a much
different organization that it was at the height of the
war. It is that Army of the early 1960s that Crumley
describes so well in this competent and engrossing
story. The characters are enlisted men and junior
officers in a security communications detachment in
the Philippines in 1962. Slag Krummel, the hero,
returns to the Army after an academic interlude, establishes personal relationships with the other soldiers,
and emerges eventually as a genuine leader. Near the
end of the book, when the detachment is sent to Vietnam, Krummel's strong body and personality enable
him to survive a harsh baptism of fire.

26.   Cunningham, Ben. Green Eyes. New York: Ballan-
       tine Books, MCMXXVI [sic; probably 1976].
       167pp.

Dubeck, a black Vietnam veteran, returns to Saigon
in 1971 in order to find his former girlfriend and a
baby son he has never seen. After a variety of experiences, he locates the woman, only to find that
she has married someone else and that his son has
died. Dubeck decides to adopt a half-black Vietnamese
orphan and take him back to America.

27.   Davis, George. Coming Home. New York: Dell
       Publishing Co. , Inc. , 1975 (© 1971). 189pp.

This novel is notable for an exploration of the relationships between black and white Air Force pilots
based in Thailand. No dates are given, but the action
takes place during attacks on Haiphong harbor. The
plot is sketchy, and narration moves from one person
to another in each chapter. The scenes of combat
flying are not as numerous as in most Air Force novels. The characters are intriguing, however, and the
setting in Thailand is described in detail.

28.   Derrig, Peter. The Pride of the Green Berets.

New York: Paperback Library, Inc., 1966.
288pp.

In the early part of the war, the Special Forces caught
the imagination of some Americans, and they were
fitting subjects for such books as this. A twelve-man
Special Forces team is active primarily in the Mekong
Delta in the early 1960s. There is a surprising
amount of accurate military detail. Among the plot
elements are U. S. -Vietnamese feuds, struggles with
cowardly and venal American officers, and the inevitable love story between the team captain and a lovely
Vietnamese woman. In one of the many battles, an
ARVN unit outfights a larger Vietcong force. Another
time, an American staff colonel stalks and kills two
Vietcong machine gunners with a knife. In line with
this sort of patriotic optimism, the book ends when
the team commander is promoted to major and awarded
the Congressional Medal of Honor.

29.   Dunn, Mary Lois.   The Man in the Box: A Story
      from Vietnam.   New York: McGraw-Hill Book
      Company, 1968.   155pp.   68-19488.

The subtitle may be a bit misleading, because there is
no evidence that the author based her book on any firsthand experience in Vietnam. An American Special
Forces man is wounded and captured by the Vietcong.
They place him in an exposed box or cage in a Montagnard village. A young boy, Chau Li, rescues the
soldier and helps him return to an American unit.
They are separated in a subsequent battle, and the
soldier is evacuated to Da Nang. The boy takes a
sampan and loyally sets off to follow him there. For
what could easily be taken as a children's story, the
descriptions of brutality and torture are quite graphic.

30.   Durden, Charles.   No Bugles, No Drums.   New York:
      The Viking Press, 1976.   287pp.   76-91.   New
      York: Charter, 1978.

Identified as a first novel on the dust wrapper, this
account of Army enlisted men at the notional Song My
Swine Project frequently attempts humor and often

achieves it. The first-person narrative is cynical and
adolescent, told by the hero, Jamie Hawkins, a young
private from Georgia. The dialogue and settings are
realistic; the characters include standard military
types--an innocent private, a tough old sergeant, and
an incompetent second lieutenant. Among the other
characters are a best buddy who is killed and a black
soldier who turns traitor. After much action and in-
action, Hawkins, hardened and embittered by the war,
murders the black turncoat and tries to walk home to
Atlanta. Of course, he only makes it to the coast.
He is finally discharged from the Army with nothing
remaining but his "unshakable bad attitude."

31.   Eastlake, William. The Bamboo Bed. New York:
          Simon and Schuster, 1969. 350pp. 70-79630.

This might well be the closest approach to a Catch-
22 of the Vietnam War. Everything is symbolic and
complex. The "Bamboo Bed" of the title is a rescue
helicopter; characters throughout recline, rest, and
fornicate on bamboo beds; and the bamboo bed probably
also stands for Vietnam. Among the most durable
characters are Captain Knightbridge and his female
aide. They copulate above battle zones in the (helicopter) bamboo bed. Eastlake certainly manages to
represent the chaos and ambiguity of Vietnam.

32.   Field, Della. Vietnam Nurse. New York: Avon
          Books, 1966. 126pp.

Nurse Lee Knight finds military service in Vietnam
to be exciting and romantic, not squalid and dangerous. She arrives in Saigon as an ensign in the Navy
Nurse Corps. Her fiance is a Green Beret officer,
missing in the jungle, and one of her purposes in
coming to Vietnam is to find him. Lee Knight gives
some perfunctory attention to her nursing duties,
which are described in the most general way, but
most of her attention must go to resisting the advances
of strong, handsome, young men. When they are not
busy "dropping from parachutes and fighting hand-to-
hand," they just cannot leave Lee alone. After learning that her fiance has been killed, Lee transfers her

affections to another Special Forces trooper and accompanies him on several adventures, including intense combat.   Her new lover is eventually wounded, but no so badly that they cannot live happily ever after.

33.   Fleming, Thomas. Officers' Wives. Garden City,
            New York: Doubleday & Company, Inc. , 1981.
            645pp.   80-1063.

Fleming writes with assurance and familiarity about military subjects as he describes the lives of four West Point graduates and their wives from 1950 through 1975.   A substantial part of the book is set in Saigon in 1963 and 1964, and it deals with the lives of U. S. Army officers and their dependents during the over-throw of the Diem government.   There are realistic scenes of terrorist attacks on American civilians, including one in which a little girl is killed.   The male characters argue various points of view about the Vietnam War and convey the impression that many professional soldiers thought the war was lost as early as the mid-1960s.   The book also describes rather despicable acts against military wives and children performed by members of the antiwar movement.

34.   Ford, Daniel. Incident at Muc Wa. Garden City,
            New York: Doubleday & Company, Inc. , 1967.
            231pp.   67-12876. New York: Pyramid Books,
            1968. New York: Jove Publications, Inc. ,
            1979. Published as Go Tell It to the Spartans.

This novel provided the basis for the motion picture of the same name as its more recent title.   Although locations and units are nominally disguised, this describes the Special Forces in the Vietnam highlands in 1964.   The establishment and subsequent loss of a fortified camp at Muc Wa proceed from the military politics of careerist officers who are unbelievable fools.   The men on the ground are more credible, although they include such standard characters as a foolish second lieutenant and a wise old sergeant. Details of locale and military matters are convincing.

35.   Gangemi, Kenneth. The Interceptor Pilot. London:
       Marion Boyars, 1980. 127pp. 79-56849.

A very potent idea is handled here in an unusual and
unsatisfying style. James Wilson, a Korean War
fighter pilot, is troubled by reports of U.S. bombing
of civilian targets in North Vietnam. Wilson resigns
his reserve commission, leaves his professorship at
the University of Colorado, and goes to Russia. There,
he is trained to fly interceptor missions against American planes over North Vietnam. After some initial
success, Wilson is shot down near Hanoi by a fighter
mission sent from a carrier specifically to kill him.
All of this is told in a literary style so economical
that it is almost barren; it might be notes for a play
or motion picture. Although this may have some experimental merit, one expects that such prose is almost as easy to write as it is to read.

36.   Garfield, Brian. The Last Bridge. New York: David
       McKay Company, Inc. , 1966. 277pp. 66-23423.

This novel of high adventure is difficult to believe,
but easy and interesting to read. In the span of a
few days, a small team of Americans and South Vietnamese plan and execute a mission into North Vietnam
to rescue an American prisoner and to destroy a vital
railroad bridge. They complete both goals successfully.
Along the way, they steal a great deal of North Vietnamese equipment; kill a number of people with explo-
sives, small arms, knives, and bare hands; and outwit
all opposing forces that have the ill luck to meet them.
Some scenes of torture are effective. The characters
are all solid military types.

37.   Giovanitti, Len. The Man Who Won the Medal of
       Honor. New York: Random House, 1973. 211pp.
       73-5003.

Giovanitti does not convey a sense of assured familiarity with the area in which his story is set. Private
David Glass is drafted and sent to Vietnam in 1968
after growing up in an orphanage. He sees Americans
murder Vietnamese prisoners and he kills the Amer-

icans in turn. There are no effective witnesses, and
he manages to get away with it and return safely to
the United States. Later, he is notified that he will
receive a Congressional Medal of Honor (for an act
he did not perform). At the awards ceremony, he
assaults the President and murders a military aide.
Glass is tried and found guilty, and as the book ends
he is in prison awaiting sentence. It is certainly in
order to point out the dehumanizing and ambivalent
aspects of the war, but this attempt is rather heavyhanded.

38. Graham, Gail. Cross-fire. New York: Pantheon
     Books, 1972. 135pp. 71-175953.

Its style suggests that this book might almost be meant
for children. An American infantryman, Harry, and
four Vietnamese children survive together for several
days in the jungle. Chapters alternately take the point
of view of each party. Although Harry can neither
speak to the children nor understand their language,
they gradually become sensitive to one another. After
this rather gentle mood is established, the book ends
surprisingly.

39. Groom, Winston. Better Times Than These. New
     York: Summit Books, 1978. 411pp. 78-4182.
     New York: Berkley, 1979.

An imagined company of the genuine 7th Infantry Division leaves for Vietnam in 1966. This is an unusual
beginning for a Vietnam novel, in that the entire unit
goes to war as a group. About a quarter of the book
describes activities on the troopship and elsewhere
prior to the group's arrival in the Ia Drang Valley.
Once there, they engage in much infantry combat and
the usual range of rear-area activities. A platoon
commander, Lt. Billy Kahn, is taken out of action to
be court-martialed for complicity in the rape of two
female Vietcong prisoners. While Kahn is gone, his
platoon and others of his company are overrun, and
there are many casualties. To silence Kahn's com-
plaints about the tactical situation in which the disaster
occurred, he is given an early discharge. This novel

has an interesting subplot about another officer and
his girlfriend at home who comes under the influence
of a professor who is active in the antiwar movement.

40.   Grossbach, Robert.   Easy and Hard Ways Out.   New
        York: Harper's Magazine Press, 1975.   245pp.
        74-4863.

Settings both in Vietnam and in the United States provide simultaneous looks at the lives of engineers working on a part for a new fighter bomber and of a pilot
flying the airplane over North Vietnam.   The character
and life of the pilot are in marked contrast to those
of the engineers, who are portrayed as weak people
doing easy jobs.   When the engineers in the United
States allow an electronic countermeasure device to
go into production with a design flaw, the pilot is
killed over North Vietnam as a direct consequence.
The different points of view hold the reader's attention, but the choppy chapters and frequent shifting of
perspective make this a difficult book to read.

41.   Halberstam, David.   One Very Hot Day.   Boston:
        Houghton Mifflin Company, 1967.   216pp.   New
        York: Avon, 1969.

This competent early novel of the war is set at a time
prior to the arrival of large numbers of American
troops.   Captain Beaupre is old for his rank and somewhat tired.   Assigned as an adviser to a Vietnamese
unit in the Mekong Delta, he finds the heat as much
of an enemy as the communists.   He fights the heat
throughout the entire day in which this story takes
place.   Among Beaupre's other enemies are the Vietnamese he advises.   He cannot understand or accept
their passive and lackadaisical approach to the war.
Thuong, a Vietnamese officer, views events and personalities differently from the American adviser.   Scenes
of combat, especially at the end of the book, are fast-
paced; the author is an able journalist.   Halberstam
manages to convey, even in 1967, a sense of the vast
complexity and essential hopelessness of Vietnam.

42.   Haldeman, Joe W.   War Year.   New York: Holt,

Rinehart and Winston, 1972. 121pp.   77-182778.
New York: Pocket Books, 1978.

John Farmer, a nineteen-year-old draftee, is sent to
the central highlands of Vietnam as a combat engineer
with the 4th Division. Farmer describes his experiences with an innocent, but not childlike, simplicity.
He makes friends, engages in battle, and is wounded.
After recovering from his wounds, Farmer is assigned
as a supply clerk in a rear area, but he fails to sa-
lute the jeep of a brigadier general and is sent back
to the field as punishment. He is killed in an ambush
while trying to clear a landing zone for a helicopter.
Throughout, Farmer is almost bewildered by his role
in the war. He is put into combat and later given
considerable responsibility with surprisingly brief
training and experience.

43.   Hancock, J. Robert. Memoirs of a Combat Corps-
       man. Santee, California: Blueboy Library,
       1976.

In this explicit homosexual paperback, the two main
characters, Guy and David, are caught behind enemy
lines sometime near the end of the war. The setting
and plot are incidental to the extensive and rather un-
imaginative sexual passages.

44.   Harper, Stephen. Live till Tomorrow. London:
       Collins, 1977. 195pp.

The chaotic conditions during the fall of Saigon in 1975
provide the setting for this story. Two former American servicemen, Barber and Ledger, have settled in
Saigon to run a successful business. As the city falls,
Ledger vanishes. Barber takes the man's large Vietnamese family through the harrowing and complicated
evacuation to Guam. This last exit of America from
Vietnam is told convincingly, with several anecdotes of
of escape by Americans and Vietnamese. Barber finally locates his lost partner in Singapore, but Ledger
is killed in a criminal gun fight. The plot is not too
plausible, but the setting and background are described
well.

45. Hasford, Gustav. The Short-Timers. New York:
       Harper and Row, 1979. 154pp. 78-4742. New
       York: Bantam, 1980.

     Violence and brutality occur in most Vietnam War
     novels, but they predominate utterly in this fast-paced
     story of Marine infantrymen set in and around Hue dur-
     ing what is certainly the 1968 Tet offensive. Descrip-
     tions of combat are graphic and detailed, although the
     extensive use of nicknames and Marine Corps slang
     sometimes makes the action hard to follow. The
     characters are completely brutalized, and death is
     everywhere. The narrator, Private Joker, has a
     fine eye for detail.

46. Hathaway, Bo. A World of Hurt. New York: Tap-
       linger Publishing Company, 1981. 318pp. 80-
       18147.

     During the Johnson administration, two men, Madsen
     and Sloane, are drafted and meet during Army train-
     ing. Although neither of them has much respect for
     military values, they volunteer for the Special Forces.
     After training, they are sent to a small camp outside
     of Nha Trang. They are sympathetic to the Montag-
     nard troops but are contemptuous of the other Viet-
     namese, who seem little interested in fighting. There
     is some combat, but no sense that a victory can be
     achieved. At the end of the book, they are near the
     end of their Army tours, and both of them are bitter
     about the experience.

47. Heinemann, Larry. Close Quarters. New York: Far-
       rar, Straus, Giroux, 1977. 336pp. 77-2245.
       New York: Popular Library, nd.

     Armored personnel carriers are used as light tanks
     in this long and realistic novel about an Army cavalry
     unit in and around Tayninh City in 1967. The hero,
     Philip Dosier, is an APC driver who describes events
     fully and well. The other main characters are hard-
     ened combat soldiers with utter contempt for officers
     and rear-area "housecats." They hate the enemy and
     fight with bravado and some success. At rest, they

despise and brutalize the South Vietnamese. A period
of rest and recreation in Japan is also described in
full detail. Unusually, this novel follows the hero
home to his family and friends. Once there, he learns
of his best friend's death back in Vietnam. Heinemann
maintains his pace and holds the reader's interest
throughout.

48.   Hempstone, Smith. A Tract of Time. Boston: Hough-
         ton Mifflin Company, 1966. 271pp. 66-11226.

In a preface, the author sets his story in 1963, before
and during the fall of the Diem government. Diem is
one of the characters, and the coup that led to his fall
is a major feature of the novel. Harry Colart is a
CIA operative working with mountain tribesmen against
the Vietcong. Colart's men are as much opposed to
the South Vietnamese government as they are to the
enemy. Theirs is only one dilemma among the mix
of confusion and conflicts in the book. Colart and
other characters are caught up in events out of their
control as the war widens almost from pressure of
its own. They are sensitive and thoughtful individuals,
and they dwell at length on a cause that they suspect
may already be lost.

49.   Hershman, Morris. Mission to Hell. New York:
         Pyramid Books, 1968. 157pp.

This Air Force novel is inaccurate in military details,
and the setting in Vietnam is described unconvincingly.
As the story follows the improbable career of a single
air crew, it touches upon such matters as cowardice,
homosexuality, racism, and aging. The crew moves
from one type of aircraft to another and to different
sorts of missions nearly every week. Flying in support of a remote fortress, they are shot down and
captured. After grim experiences in a North Vietnamese prison camp, most of them escape. They are
helped in part by one of their number who establishes
a homosexual liaison with one of the guards.

50.   Honig, Louis. For Your Eyes Only: Read and Destroy.

Los Angeles: Charles Pub. Co. , 1972.   249pp.
72-83313. New York: Bantam, 1973.

In a preface, the author explains that a private plan
for peace in Vietnam in the late 1960s did, in fact,
exist.   In his novel, the plan is offered by Peters,
an important international political columnist.   This
individual manages to enter the secret underground
headquarters of the National Liberation Front in South
Vietnam to present his ideas.   On the way out, he is
ambushed by agents of the CIA and of the Communist
Chinese intelligence service, each acting separately.
Along with this sort of action, the book offers discussions of the views and positions of the numerous parties to the Vietnam War in the 1960s.

51.   Huggett, William Turner. Body Count. New York:
        G. P. Putnam's Sons, 1973.   445pp.   72-97297.
        New York: Dell, 1978.

Because of its superior literary quality and historical
accuracy, Body Count must be among the very best
novels of Marines in Vietnam.   The hero is Lieutenant Chris Hawkins, an infantry platoon leader who
learns his profession at Khe Sanh, Da Nang, and elsewhere.   Woven into one long, able story are such matters as morale, race relations, military professional-
ism and careerism, and the hostile countryside of
Vietnam.   Other members of Hawkin's platoon and
company appear as interesting, individualized characters, and their actions and dialogue are credible.
At the end of the book, Hawkins leads and survives
his greatest battle and he appears to be in line for
promotion to company commander.

52.   Hunter, Evan. Sons. Garden City, New York:
        Doubleday & Company, Inc. , 1969.   396pp.
        78-79415. London: Constable, 1970.

The story of Wat Tyler alternates, chapter by chapter,
with those of his father and grandfather as each man
fights the war of his generation--World War I, World
War II, and Vietnam.   Wat is in high school in 1963,
and the portions of the novel that deal with him take

him through entering college at Yale, a romance, and
involvement with the peace movement before he is
drafted in 1965 and sent to Vietnam as an infantryman. There are scenes set in Saigon, in the jungle,
and elsewhere. Tyler's buddies represent typical
Vietnam soldiers' backgrounds and attitudes, and their
varying fates are also typical. This war-by-war com-
parison is an effective, but somewhat mechanical,
method to illustrate the attitudes of American soldiers
over the course of this century.

53.   Hynd, Noel. Revenge. New York: The Dial Press,
      1976. 275pp. 75-34127. New York: Dell,
      1978.

Only the first ten pages of this gripping novel are set
in Vietnam, but they are enough, for they describe the
brutal torture that was a feature of imprisonment in
North Vietnam. Richard Silva, an Air Force lieutenant, is tormented, and his friends are killed, by a
European guard. They believe he is French. After
release in 1973, Silva begins a hunt for the man,
which involves several interesting subplots and eventually takes him to Paris. It develops that the guard
is a French intelligence agent, and Silva has the sat-
isfaction of killing him before a final surprise at the
book's end. The very short chapters do not enhance
readability.

54.   James, Allston. Attic Light. Santa Barbara, Cal-
      ifornia: Capra Press, 1979. 96pp. 78-31541.

This short book begins in Vietnam when the hero, a
lieutenant serving as a forward artillery observer, is
badly wounded in the leg. He comes to growing con-
sciousness as he is evacuated through several hospitals
back to the United States. When the lieutenant attempts to resume his former life in an unnamed city
in the South, he encounters many problems adjusting
to civilian life. He is alienated from the people he
loved and from the institutions he understood before
he went to war. After he receives news of his best
friend's death in Vietnam, he departs for Europe.

55.   Joss, John. Sierra Sierra. Los Altos, California:
       The Soaring Press, 1977. 200pp. 77-82561.
       New York: William Morrow and Company, Inc.,
       1978.

       On the surface, this is a first-person present-tense
       novel about a record-attempt glider flight from Mount
       Olympus, Washington, to Yuma, Arizona. The pilot,
       Mark Lewis, is a retired Marine aviator who served
       in Vietnam. As the glider journey progresses, Lewis
       recalls in great detail a combat mission in Vietnam
       during which his best friend was killed. This descrip-
       tion of the employment of carrier-based F4 Phantom
       fighters against hostile ground targets is complex, but
       Joss manages all the technical information in a lucid
       and understandable manner. He is equally convincing
       in developing the character of Lewis as a career mil-
       itary pilot. Other parts of the book, not specific to
       Vietnam, are also handled adroitly.

56.   Just, Ward. Stringer. Boston: Little, Brown and
       Company, 1974. 199pp. 73-13682.

       Vietnam is not named, but it is obviously the locale
       where Stringer, a civilian, and Price, an Army offi-
       cer, are sent far into enemy territory to plant elec-
       tronic sensors along an infiltration route. There is
       friction between the two men because of their differ-
       ent backgrounds and attitudes. Descriptions of their
       equipment, movements, and surrounding jungle are
       minute. After their sensors guide in an air strike,
       Price is killed and Stringer begins to walk out. At
       this stage, about halfway through, there is a marked
       change in the literary style as the meaning of the
       novel becomes much more elusive. Stringer encoun-
       ters the enemy and his old friends in scenes that may
       be hallucinatory, and the conclusion is vague. Dia-
       logue is sometimes indicated by dashes rather than
       quotation marks, and there is a minor technical error
       in which "clip" is used incorrectly for "magazine."
       Nonetheless, Just is a good writer, and this is a pro-
       vocative view of the actions and motives of men at
       war.

57.   Kalb, Bernard, and Marvin Kalb. The Last Ambassa-

dor. Boston: Little, Brown and Company, 1981.
276pp. 81-8259.

The authors bring a wealth of experience in Vietnam
to this novel of the fall of Saigon in 1975. Hadden
Walker, the last American ambassador to South Vietnam, believes that American honor and policy will
best be served by continuing support of the South Vietnamese government. To achieve his ends, he acts
contrary to the official policy of the United States and,
indeed, contrary to the facts. Unfortunately for Walker, the communist military forces are too strong, and
the ARVN is too weak to change history. In the chaos
of the last days at the American embassy, his attempts
to negotiate with the North Vietnamese are futile and
his attempt to force the hand of the American president fails. In the end, he is evacuated against his
will. A surprise climax adds little to this engrossing
story.

58.   Kempley, Walter. The Invaders. New York: Dell,
         1979 (© 1976). 288pp.

The continental United States becomes an extended
theater of operations for the Vietnam War in this
mass-market paperback. A gang of black Army deserters in Saigon is recruited by a fanatical North
Vietnamese major to launch unauthorized rocket and
mortar attacks on targets in the U.S. They are pur-
sued by Lt. Gerald Skilling, the commander of an
improbably independent Army unit assigned to track
deserters. The deserters are paid in heroin, and
some of the action takes place in the French criminal underground. These descriptions of black-market
and smuggling activities are interesting, but they are
written so simply that they defy belief. For example,
in the nine pages after he is introduced, Eddie Pal-
mer, a deserter, joins a criminal gang in Saigon,
singlehandedly salvages their inept hijacking of a truck,
sells its contents to a Vietnamese thief he meets by
accident, kills the gang boss with one shot in the chest,
and takes over as leader. Most other action is sim-
ilarly compressed in a story that seems to take place
between 1968 and 1971. The end comes after a gunfight in New York City.

59.   Kim, Samuel. The American POWs. Boston: Bran-
      den Press, 1979. 273pp. 77-90036.

      Like its author, the hero of this novel is a Korean-
      American. Much of the book is an unrelenting ac-
      count of deplorable conditions and unspeakable brutality
      in a Vietcong jungle prison camp. With the help of a
      beautiful woman doctor who decides to defect from the
      Vietcong, the hero escapes and returns to an American
      unit after an adventuresome journey through the jungle.
      Both the narration and dialogue are artificial and un-
      necessarily structured. The novel is difficult to follow
      and to believe. Also, there are numerous mistakes
      about weapons and other military details.

60.   Kirkwood, James. Some Kind of Hero. New York:
      Thomas Y. Crowell Company, 1975. 399pp.
      75-5725. New York: New American Library,
      1976.

      Eddie Keller is a long-suffering hero. As a child,
      Eddie is abandoned by his father to the care of an
      alcoholic mother. Later, he is drafted into the Army
      and sent to Vietnam, leaving behind his new, pregnant
      wife. Eddie is captured and held prisoner in Hanoi
      for five years. The lengthy prison-camp sequences
      deal fluently with physical and mental torture, homo-
      sexuality, betrayal, and death, yet they lack a hard
      edge of realism. Eddie returns home to find that
      his wife has squandered his back pay and moved in
      with her former lover. His mother has had a stroke,
      and he must face her medical bills. After an at-
      tempted reconciliation with his father fails, Eddie
      turns to crime and eventually becomes a competent
      armed robber. Throughout it all, he maintains an
      amazing equanimity.

61.   Klose, Kevin, and Philip A. McCombs. The Typhoon
      Shipments. New York: W. W. Norton & Com-
      pany, Inc., 1974. 280pp.

      Bodies of deceased American servicemen are used to
      convey heroin from South Vietnam to the United States
      in this fast-paced thriller. The principal characters

are customs agents in pursuit of the smugglers.
Some of the action is set in Washington, D.C., and
elsewhere, but there are many scenes in Saigon and
one account of an improbable combat assault. Belief
is also strained by the prospect of the body of a U.S.
senator's son lying in the Capitol Rotunda full of heroin. This is followed by a wild gunfight in Arlington
National Cemetery. While the essential story is not
believable, the characters and their dialogue are.

62.   Kolpacoff, Victor. The Prisoners of Quai Dong.
       New York: New American Library, 1967.
       214pp. 67-25937.

Biographical material at the end of the book establishes
that Kolpacoff has not been to Vietnam, and there is
no mention of his having had military service. That
may account for the minor inaccuracies in his novel
about soldiers in Vietnam. Kreuger, a former infantry lieutenant, is imprisoned at Quai Dong, on the
South China Sea, for refusing to fight. After a year
at hard labor, he is told to use his Vietnamese-language
skill to question a Vietcong suspect. The interrogation
and ancillary torture of the suspect occupy most of
the book. Kreuger struggles with the prisoner, the
other Americans, and with himself and his values.
In the end, he stops the torture with an inspired lie,
claiming that the prisoner named a location for enemy
supplies. By utter accident, when troops are sent,
they draw fire and find supplies. Kreuger is released
from the stockade as a reward for his supposed good
service.

63.   Krueger, Carl. Wings of the Tiger. New York:
       Frederick Fell, Inc., 1966. 285pp. 66-27604.

In lengthy prefatory material, Krueger recounts his
long association with the Air Force as a novelist and
screenwriter. He explains that Wings of the Tiger
began life as a screenplay. The novel, written in
superlatives, certainly reflects its origin. Aircraft
are described in very great detail, both at rest and
in battle. The human characters are bantering, coura-
geous pilots, bent on their mission to destroy an airfield north of Hanoi. Subplots include romance, spies,

and a look at the lives of some amazingly simpleminded North Vietnamese living near the intended
target. In view of subsequent events, Krueger's
bright enthusiasm for the war seems naive, but his
skill as a writer holds the story together.

64.   Larson, Charles. The Chinese Game. Philadelphia:
          J. B. Lippincott Company, 1969. 236pp. 69-
          11308.

The central character of this complicated and somewhat vague novel is Belgard, a Special Forces captain who commands a Montagnard camp in 1963.
Wounded in battle, he is evacuated to a hospital.
Belgard's main interest seems to be to protect his
camp from both the Vietcong and the South Vietnamese military politicians. In pursuit of this, he is
drawn into a conflict between Diem and the Buddhists
and into a love affair with a Vietnamese woman. Elements of dreams or hallucinations are woven into the
story. Belgard finally ends up in the city of Hue,
where his story ends in a curious and unsatisfying
fashion.

65.   Littell, Robert. Sweet Reason. Boston: Houghton
          Mifflin Company, 1974. 210pp. 73-12079.
          New York: Popular Library, 1976.

This is one of the rare Navy novels of Vietnam.
During only three days off the coast of Vietnam, the
World War II destroyer Eugene F. Ebersole sinks
both an innocent junk and a ditched aircraft; it attacks a school of whales with depth charges and
causes the destruction of a friendly village. The
characters are written in a way that suggests the
author has anti-military attitudes. Regular officers
and loyal sailors are incompetent fools; pacifists
among the officers and crew are portrayed as interesting, sincere idealists. "Sweet Reason, " an anony-
mous pamphleteer, urges resistance to military au-
thority, and eventually the men at the guns refuse to
fire. Shortly afterward, the Ebersole collides with
an aircraft carrier and sinks with half the men aboard.
Littell's humor is often effective, as when he exagger-

ates the hostile posturing of black militants among the
crew, but the short chapters and subchapters tend to
divide the text awkwardly.

66.   Little, Loyd. Parthian Shot. New York: The Viking
       Press, 1975 (© 1973). 278pp. 74-30250.

This sensitive and somewhat gentle novel is written
by a former Special Forces medic with service in
Vietnam. It is set among the Hao Hao Buddhist sect
in the Mekong Delta in 1964. Several members of a
Special Forces team are lost on official Army records
and temporarily stranded in their area of operations
by seasonal floods. They decide to stay on and work
for the local political and military leader. The characters are credible, even the old-time sergeant and
the incompetent lieutenant. In contrast to novels set
later in the war, relations between Americans and
Vietnamese are excellent. There are fine elements
of humor, including the formation of a joint stock
company with the Vietcong as both customers and
shareholders and the implementation of a Rand Insti-
tute recommendation that the Hao Hao survive the war
by pretending to support both sides. Action is somewhat slow for a war story, and combat is confined to
patrol skirmishes. Eventually, some of the soldiers
decide to return to the Army and to the U.S. while
others remain in the village. In a final chapter, almost an afterword, the village is destroyed by an air
attack some years after the main action occurs.

67.   Louang, Phou. The Men of Company 97. np: Neo
       Lao Haksat Publications, 1971. 61pp.

The men of Company 97 carry true revolutionary
spirit in their hearts. They fight the Yankee aggressors and their Lao lackeys with commitment, skill,
and inevitable success. They love their homeland
and have an excellent relationship with the peasants.
Subordinate fighters are prompt and alert to take correct political and military instruction from their superiors. When not actually fighting or engaging in
political discussions, the men have time for a hint
of romance and even a song or two about the revolu-

tion. Physically, the book reflects rather primitive
origins and a certain unfamiliarity with common English usage.

68.   McCarry, Charles. The Tears of Autumn. New
           York: Saturday Review Press, 1975 (© 1974).
           276pp. 74-7419.

The premise of this unusual novel is that the assassination of President John Kennedy was arranged by
the extended family of Vietnamese leader Diem in re-
taliation for Kennedy's presumed complicity in the
1963 coup that led to Diem's death. The hero is
Paul Christopher, a senior and romantic American
intelligence agent. He works out the puzzle as he
travels through Europe, Africa, and Southeast Asia.
Christopher pursues leads, questions other agents,
and tortures informants. He learns, among other
things, that the Russians had Lee Harvey Oswald
killed by Jack Ruby because they feared unjustified
blame for Kennedy's assassination. When Christopher
presents his conclusions and supporting documentation
to aides of President Johnson, they suppress the information because they fear its release would undermine
popular American support for the war. The settings
all appear accurate, and the novel contains information about the Vietnamese kinship system.

69.   McQuinn, Donald E. Targets. New York: Macmillan
           Publishing Co., Inc., 1980. 499pp. 79-25493.

Vietnamese characters play a large part in this novel,
which is set in Saigon in 1969. Charles Taylor, a
Marine Corps major near retirement, joins a small
intelligence and security unit that is staffed by Vietnamese and by Americans from both the Army and
the Marines. The complex plot centers on an attempt
to capture Binh, a gunrunner and black-market operator who supplies American weapons to the Vietcong.
The characters engage in fraud, sabotage, torture,
and murder as they pursue Binh and other criminals.
Throughout, there is a sense among them that the
war is already lost. But, in the end, Taylor causes
Binh to be captured through the employment of a cruel

but effective ruse. Taylor leaves Vietnam for retirement in America. There are few scenes of combat
in the field, but the book describes much of the civilian and rear-echelon environment in Vietnam.

70. Maitland, Derek. The Only War We've Got. New
York: William Morrow and Company, Inc.,
1970. 270pp. 70-128764. London: New Authors Ltd., 1970

Maitland is a British journalist who worked in Vietnam prior to the 1968 Tet offensive. Representations
of that offensive and of other major battles provide
much of what plot there is in this humorous and ironi-
cal book. In thin disguises, the major personalities,
groups, institutions, and events of the Vietnam War
of that time appear here, and they all are portrayed
as being without sense or honor. Favorite targets of
ridicule are Americans, but all characters, including
the Vietcong and a British newspaperman, are touched
by Maitland's consistently acid wit. An important
battle at the end of the book takes place in a huge
American Post Exchange where everyone involved is
more interested in loot or profit than in military victory. Realistic scenes of bloody death occur occasionally as abrupt surprises amid the otherwise unrelent-
ing satire.

71. Martin, Ian Kennedy. Rekill. New York: Ballantine
Books, 1978 © 1977). 217pp. 77-7646.

Numerous technical mistakes about weapons, military
slang, nomenclature, radio procedure, and rock climb-
ing combine with questionable grammar and unusual
capitalization to suggest that this mass-market paperback may have been written and edited in some haste.
The plot has to do with a 1968 massacre of Vietnamese civilians and the vendetta, some eight years later,
of a North Vietnamese major against the guilty American officers. One of the subplots deals with interne-
cine struggles among different intelligence agencies.
Action takes place also in Albania, where a political
assassination incidentally destroys a Chinese missile
base! The characters are neither memorable nor

credible, but Martin does describe fast action well,
and the revenge theme is handled strongly throughout.

72.   Meyer, Nicholas.   Target Practice.   New York: Pin-
           nacle Books, 1974. 186pp.

This detective story set in the early 1970s touches
upon several Vietnam issues.   A former prisoner of
war commits suicide after being charged with collaboration by another prisoner.   A private detective is
hired to investigate the charges.   He learns of the
dead man's training, combat experience, and imprisonment through interviews with former soldiers.   There
is one chilling session in a veterans' hospital with an
armless, legless survivor.   The story that emerges
is that the former prisoners had been involved in a
massacre of innocent civilians prior to their capture
by the North Vietnamese.

73.   Moore, Gene D.   The Killing at Ngo Tho.   New York:
           W. W. Norton & Company, Inc., 1967.   242pp.
           67-12445.

Like his hero, Scott Leonard, Moore is a regular
Army colonel with service in Vietnam.   Leonard is
assigned as an adviser to the Vietnamese chief of a
province on the Cambodian border.   There is a bit
of internal trouble with dates, but this seems to be
set in the mid-1960s, just after the termination of
the Diem government.   There is not as much pessim-
ism and cynicism here as in later novels.   Leonard
has the motives and talents of an ambitious professional officer.   Some of his Vietnamese counterparts
are capable patriots, the peasants are loyal, and the
cause is not yet lost.   Colonel Leonard's particular
adventure has to do with the location and destruction
of a concealed Vietcong headquarters.   He also feuds
with an irrational superior officer.   The ending, like
the whole book, is optimistic.

74.   Moore, Robin.   The Green Berets.   New York:
           Crown Publishers, Inc., 1965.   341pp.   65-15849.
           New York: Avon, 1966.   New York: Crown

Publishers, Inc., 1969 (limited edition for the
Green Beret Holding Corporation).

One of the earlier novels about Americans fighting in
Vietnam, this enthusiastic account of Special Forces
adventures is the basis for the motion picture of the
same name. Captain Steve Kornie and his team are
clearly the good guys, and the Vietcong and North
Vietnamese are just as clearly and wholly bad. The
plot is actually a series of separate stories, which
include the brilliant defense of a Special Forces camp
and a clandestine operation inside North Vietnam.
Moore is convinced, it seems, that the Special Forces
will win the war, despite only lukewarm assistance
from the South Vietnamese and restrictions imposed by
higher military and civilian command.

75.   Moore, Robin, with June Collins. The Khaki Mafia.
           New York: Crown Publishers, Inc., 1971.
           284pp. 79-168317. New York: Avon, 1972.

Corruption of high-ranking Army sergeants who ran
recreational clubs in Vietnam and elsewhere among
American forces became known to the public in the
late 1960s and early 1970s. This fictionalized account
of those events reflects Moore's close familiarity with
the U.S. Army. Although the plot and action are simplified, the details and dialogue ring true, and the
extent of the fraud and theft is staggering. June Collins entertained in clubs in Vietnam and gained firsthand experience at a number of activities that must
have enhanced her contribution to the book. Little
in this novel reveals the anguish and doubts about the
war that are so common in other works.

76.   Moore, Robin, and Henry Rothblatt. Court Martial.
           Garden City, New York: Doubleday and Company,
           Inc., 1971. 410pp. 75-139048.

This story of the killing of a suspected Vietnamese
double agent by Army Special Forces officers is set
both in Vietnam and in Washington, D.C. Details
of the alleged crime emerge in chapters and sections
that alternate with those describing the investigation
and other subsequent events. Rivalries between reg-

ular Army officers and the Special Forces play an
important part in the novel, as do conflicts between
American and Vietnamese political factions. The hero
is Hank McEwan, an attorney, and much of the second
half of the book describes a military trial in which he
ultimately succeeds on behalf of the accused officers.

77. Morris, Edita. Love to Vietnam. New York: Monthly
        Review Press, 1968. 92pp. 68-22425.

What this Swedish author has to say, simply and
rather crudely, is that Americans burn Asians. The
story unfolds in letters written by a young Japanese
man who was disfigured and orphaned at Nagasaki.
He writes first to a young girl in Vietnam who has
been burned by American napalm. Then he visits
her there and describes his adventures to a friend
in Japan. These are such loving and exquisite vic-
tims that they seem to exist only to suffer from American bombing.

78. Morris, Jim. Strawberry Soldier. New York: Ace
        Books, 1972. 237pp.

Perhaps the most marginal work in this list, this is
more a story of a returned veteran. Several flashback scenes are, however, set in the Vietnam highlands, where the narrator was a Special Forces officer working with Montagnard tribesmen. His reaction
and adjustment to civilian life are colored utterly by
his Vietnam experience. Other veterans appear as
important characters in the book. The story has to
do with narcotics dealing, skydiving under the influence
of LSD, and the promotion of rock concerts. In the
context of its setting in the late 1960s or early 1970s,
the book is entertaining and believable. Morris has a
fine, alert writing style.

79. Morrison, C. T. The Flame in the Icebox. New
        York: Exposition Press, 1968. 112pp.

This brief novel offers an unfortunate and unusual com-
bination of florid descriptive prose and oversimplified

characters and action. An American infantry squad
(which is led, implausibly, by a lieutenant) spends a
day in heavy combat with the Vietcong. After ambush
and counterambush, most of the men are killed. Two
enlisted men are captured and taken to a camp in the
nearby jungle. During their captivity, the men are
treated reasonably well, and some attempt is made
by their captors to indoctrinate them. After one or
two halfhearted attempts at escape fail, the men are
told that they will be released soon in any case. Then
American forces attack the camp and kill everyone,
including the prisoners. The book concludes with the
helpful explanation that Vietnam is the flame in the
icebox of the Cold War. The review copy is badly
made; the stitching on the spine is incomplete.

80.   Myrer, Anton. Once an Eagle. New York: Holt,
         Rinehart and Winston, 1968. 881pp. New York:
         Berkley, 1977.

Myrer's "Khotiane" is a country very similar to Vietnam. Chapters relating to it appear at the end of this
lengthy novel about two career Army officers between
World War I and 1962. Sam Damon is clearly a good
guy, and Courtney Massengale is unquestionably a bad
one, yet both rise to be generals. Sam Damon is
called out of retirement to evaluate the military
situation in Khotiane, where Massengale commands
American advisers. Damon's honest appraisal does
not fit with Massengale's plans to bring in large numbers of American combat troops and perhaps to invade
China. In the end, however, it appears that evil triumphs over good, because Damon is killed and Massengale is left alive with his plans. The characters
are a bit too pure to be wholly believable, but Myrer
offers an intriguing suggestion of how the Vietnam war
might have been viewed by senior military officers.

81.   Nagel, William. The Odd Angry Shot. Sydney: Angus
         and Robertson, 1979 (© 1975). 98pp.

The Australian contribution in Vietnam is not well
known to Americans. As portrayed here, their soldiers had much the same experiences and attitudes

as ours. The narrator and his comrades are members of the Australian Army's elite SAS unit, similar to American Special Forces or Rangers. Their attitudes about the war and their part in it are cynical and sarcastic. The Australians have generally friendly encounters with the Americans they encounter. They detest both the South Vietnamese and the peace demonstrators back home. There are a few errors missed in proofreading and an unusual physical layout. This edition has still photographs from a motion picture based on the novel.

82.   Nahum, Lucien. Shadow 81. London: New English
            Library, 1976 (© 1975). 285pp.

This is an account of an imaginative crime committed in the context of the Vietnam War. An Air Force general conspires with the pilot of an experimental fighter bomber to fake a crash during an exciting mission over Hanoi. The pilot then transports the plane on a specially constructed ship to North America, where he uses it to threaten a commercial airliner and extort a large ransom. The pilot returns to Vietnam and arranges to be captured by the North Vietnamese. After enduring five months of captivity, the pilot is released at the end of the war, and he and the general escape with their loot. Almost like human characters, airplanes and their capabilities are described in loving detail.

83.   Nelson, Charles. The Boy Who Picked the Bullets
            Up. New York: William Morrow and Company,
            Inc., 1981. 420pp. 81-9438.

Kurt Strom is a Navy medic serving with the Marines in Vietnam in 1966 and 1967. Strom, a homosexual, tells the story of his service in letters home to several friends. His work as a medic involves some of the bloodiest and most realistic action that appears in any Vietnam War novel. There are also frequent accounts of sexual activities that suggest that homosexuality was at least on the scene among American forces in Vietnam. Strom is wounded twice, and when he returns home he is addicted to morphine. Nelson

is an able writer; this is a book with a unique point
of view.

84.   Newhafer, Richard. No More Bugles in the Sky.
        New York: New American Library, 1966.
        206pp. 66-22216.

        Like other Air Force novelists, Newhafer suffers from
        no lack of imagination and enthusiasm. His hero, Dan
        Belden, is a World War II and Korean War ace on a
        semi-secret mission for the Director of the CIA in
        1964. Belden's job is to use air power to widen the
        Vietnam War! Only then can enough American troops
        be brought in to win it. Belden's adventures are
        numerous. Often he is in the cockpit, flying against
        an old Chinese foe from Korea. Finally, Belden is
        successful, and the President authorizes the dispatch
        of one hundred thousand American troops to Vietnam.
        In view of the subsequent developments in the Viet-
        nam War, Newhafer's ideas of 1966 are unfortunately
        prophetic.

85.   O'Brien, Tim. Going After Cacciato. New York:
        Delacorte Press, 1978. 338pp. New York:
        Delta, 1979. 77-11723.

        This complex and deep novel won a National Book
        Award in 1978 and has been very favorably reviewed
        in major journals. Cacciato, an infantryman, walks
        away from the Vietnam battlefield heading for Paris
        overland. Other members of his platoon pursue him
        through Southeast Asia, the Middle East, and Europe.
        Chapters describing the chase alternate with others
        that flash back to realistic infantry action in the war.
        In addition to the surface story, the book deals with
        the effect of war on men and with human morality in
        a more obscure manner.

86.   Pelfrey, William. The Big V. New York: Liveright,
        1972. 158pp. 78-167289.

        This is one of the most touching and complete novels
        of the Army infantry in the Vietnam War. The hero,

Henry Winsted, is a draftee assigned as a radio
operator with the 4th Division in the Central Highlands of Vietnam. The action takes place at the
height of American involvement in the war. Winsted
has typical experiences in training, in base camp,
and in combat in the field. The other characters,
mostly enlisted men and junior officers, are complete
and convincing. Pelfrey writes dialogue well, and the
conversations are spontaneous and natural. Senior
NCOs and officers contend with the poor morale of
draftees, but all of the soldiers have a measure of
pride in their fighting ability. The review copy has
a very small typeface, a bothersome mechanical flaw
in a fine novel.

87.   Pollock, Lawrence. Xin Loi (Sorry About That) Doc!
            New York: Vantage Press, 1971. 379pp.

These anecdotes about the 55th Evacuation Hospital
near Qui Nhon are set at a time when American
troops are on hand in large numbers. The author is
clearly not a conventional novelist. There are numerous curiosities of format and style. The medical action is fascinating and realistic, although somewhat
brutal. There is also an oppressive vulgarity in the
characters' action and language. In a body of literature notable for awful people and scenes, this book
stands out. One doctor, for instance, extracts his
payment for a nurse's abortion in the form of inter-
course in advance on the operating table. More editing or an able joint author could have turned this
potent material into a much more readable book.

88.   Porter, John B. If I Make My Bed in Hell. Waco,
            Texas: World Books, Publishers, 1969. 165pp.
            69-20234.

In a prefatory note, Porter explains his own experiences as an Army chaplain in Vietnam as the basis
for his novel. Chaplain Grayson is a character much
like Porter. He serves both in the field and in camp
with an airborne infantry unit near Saigon. He deals
with soldiers' moral, psychological, and religious
problems, and with his own doubts and fears. There

is no question about Porter's sincerity. His writing
ability is generally equal to his task, although characters and their conversations are rather obviously
constructed and the ending is rather abrupt. This
thorough view of the life of an Army chaplain is
unique among Vietnam War novels.

89.   Pratt, John Clark. The Laotian Fragments. New
            York: The Viking Press, 1974. 245pp. 73-
            2499.

The "fragments" of the title are fictitious letters,
memoranda, military reports, diaries, orders, and
transcriptions that comprise the book and tell the
story of U.S. Air Force "civilian" pilots in Laos in
the mid-1960s. The epistolary style presents some
problems; readers familiar with military communications will be able to follow the story, but others may
not. The main character, Major William Blake, is
one of several American pilots who appear actually to
be running the Laotian air force in its battles with
communist forces and various political armies. The
plot, characters, and action sequences are not over-
done, as is so often the case in Air Force novels,
but are vivid and convincing. The author, a former
Air Force pilot in Laos, has been instrumental in
building the Vietnam War Collection at Colorado State
University, upon which this bibliography is based.
This is certainly the most mature and able Air Force
novel of the war.

90.   Rivers, Gayle, and James Hudson. The Five Fingers.
            Garden City, New York: Doubleday & Company,
            Inc., 1978. 280pp. 77-80910. New York:
            Bantam, 1979.

The title is the code name for a five-man team of
various nationalities that is infiltrated through Laos
and Vietnam into Southern China in 1969. The first-
person narrative is provided by Warrant Officer Rivers,
who is presumably the author of the same name. The
book was probably "told to" the other author, and that
may account for the awkward phrasing of the action
sequences, e.g., "He was bleeding from every possible

direction." Descriptions of logistics and equipment
throughout are quite detailed, and the infiltration sequences occupy most of the novel prior to the chaotic
conclusion. At least one of the authors clearly knows
his ground, but the effect of the collaboration is uncon-
vincing.

91.   Roberts, Suzanne. Vietnam Nurse. New York: Ace
            Books, Inc., 1966. 142pp.

This view of the Vietnam War as the locale for a
sort of extended prom date is certainly unusual, even
in a varied and unconventional body of literature.
Nurse Katie arrives in Vietnam with the personality
of a high school virgin. The settings in Vietnam and
indeed in the Army are perfunctory and entirely notional. The war appears as occasional bursts of ma-
chine-gun fire from bothersome snipers. These may
interrupt Katie and her beau of the moment, but they
represent no real danger. Several other novels about
nurses by the same author are listed on one of the
preliminary pages. This one reveals little or nothing
about medical care in Vietnam.

92.   Roth, Robert. Sand in the Wind. Boston: Little,
            Brown and Company, 1973. 498pp. 73-8768.
            New York: Pinnacle, 1974.

Murder, rape, cannibalism, racial tension, war resistance, and startling humor appear in this long novel
along with the more traditional aspects of Marine infantry at war. The action is set in and around Hue
in what is clearly the 1968 Tet offensive. The main
characters are Kramer, a lieutenant, and Chalice, an
enlisted man. The relationships between them and
the other characters are realistic and well written.
Characters have convincing personal mannerisms, personalities, and conversations. There are many scenes
of small-unit action, and the entire book seems credible and convincing. Roth's literary style is able
enough to maintain a reader's interest and to convey
and sustain the emotional environment of war.

93.   Rowe, John. Count Your Dead. Sydney: Angus and
           Robertson, 1968. 223pp.

       Incompetent American and Vietnamese officers do a
       bad job of implementing a stupid strategy in this novel
       of an Army brigade in Duc Binh province. Bill Mor-
       gan, a staff major with recent combat experience,
       finds himself in constant conflict with his commanding
       officer, a colonel who is interested in his own career.
       Together with Vietnamese officers, the colonel involves
       the brigade in several pointless battles that cause
       heavy casualties. At one point, the colonel inflates
       an actual enemy body count of twenty-three to the im-
       probable figure of five hundred. Morgan's colleagues
       have typically low opinions of the South Vietnamese
       and of the American peace movement. Eventually,
       the colonel's "capacity to put an exaggeratedly favor-
       able interpretation on events" brings him promotion
       to general, while Morgan is fired from his job and
       sent to a desk in Saigon.

94.   Rubin, Jonathon. The Barking Deer. New York:
           George Braziller, 1974. 335pp. 73-88042.

       Rubin describes a situation so confused, corrupt, and
       tragic that it would be unbelievable in any modern
       context other than that of the Vietnam War. His story
       is set among Montagnard tribesmen and an American
       Special Forces team during the mid-1960s. Most of
       the action and conversations occur among the Montag-
       nards, and the impression is conveyed that they are
       separated from Americans by cultural differences too
       great to understand, much less to breach. The com-
       plexity of characters, spirit relationships, and folk
       activities is difficult and sometimes burdensome to
       follow. The American characters are officers and
       enlisted men of the Special Forces team, and at the
       end of this extremely involved novel, they are among
       the many dead.

95.   Runyon, Charles W. Bloody Jungle. New York:
           Ace Books, Inc., 1966. 157pp.

       Lieutenant Clay Macklin is a one-man army. A Green

Beret stationed in Vietnam in the early 1960s, he
survived the destruction of his camp, escapes through
the jungle with the help of a Vietnamese woman, saves
the wife of a French plantation owner from gang rape
by the Vietcong, and makes his way alone to another
Special Forces camp. Macklin is evacuated to Saigon,
where he receives a Silver Star, engages in some
freehand spying, survives another terrific fight in
the jungle, destroys the secret headquarters of the
Vietcong, and rescues some prisoners in the process.
To achieve all this, Lt. Macklin triumphs over the
jungle, the enemy, the corrupt South Vietnamese, inept officers in his own army, and the world press.
Everything happens in less than one month, and that
is hard to believe.

96.   Sadler, Barry. Casca: The Eternal Mercenary.
                New York: Charter, 1979. 246pp.

This supernatural story opens in Nha Trang, Vietnam,
in 1970. A wounded Army sergeant in a military hospital begins to heal himself of wounds that his doctors
believe to be fatal. It develops that the sergeant is
nothing less than an ancient and eternal soldier. As
a Roman legionnaire, he thrust his spear into the side
of Christ on the Cross and was doomed to an everlast-
ing life of battle. Most of the action takes place in
Imperial Rome, and the historical detail is sparse but
accurate. At the end of the novel, the sergeant and
all of his records disappear from the hospital in Vietnam, and he is seen again fighting in the Israeli army.

97.   Sadler, Barry. The Moi. Nashville, Tennessee:
                Aurora Publishers, Inc., 1977. 214pp. 75-
                26255.

Sadler, a former Green Beret and Vietnam veteran,
certainly knows that the Russian Tokarev pistol used
in Vietnam is a semi-automatic, not a revolver. That,
however, is the only mistake in a book replete with
technical information. The story concerns Lim, a
fanatical North Vietnamese major, and Reider, an
American Special Forces sergeant who is his prisoner.
Lim tortures Reider for what seem to be months in

an effort to break his spirit and reduce him to a
"moi"--an animal. Reider resists until he can achieve
what is for him a heroic climax. While revealing
much of Lim's and Reider's thoughts and reflections,
Sadler manages to keep them separate and distinct.
The premise of this story is a bit strained, but it is
a gripping adventure.

98.   Sanders, Pamela. Miranda. Boston: Little, Brown
       and Company, 1978. 429pp. 78-18911.

The title of this long and literate novel is the first
name of its heroine, a freelance journalist. The
story moves frequently between the present and the
past, with complicated plots in all times. The Vietnam sections occur in 1962 and 1963. They appear
to be based on accurate memory of firsthand experience. Moving around in Southeast Asia, Miranda
gains access to American military officers (and to
many other men) by allowing them access to her body.
Her adventures in a mountain Special Forces camp
are supported by careful and detailed cultural background on the local population. American characters
encountered at this early period of the war evince an
aggressive attitude and a belief in eventual victory.

99.   Sloan, James Park. War Games. Boston: Houghton
       Mifflin, 1971. 186pp. 77-124357.

When a first-person novel takes the form of a diary,
it usually has the advantages of a simple chronological
progression, a consistent point of view, and some insight into at least one of the characters (the diarist).
In this story, the chronology is steady, but the point
of view and the personality of the chief character are
elusive. The hero is assigned to an Army unit in the
Mekong Delta, which apparently symbolizes, rather
than describes, the real Army. The persons he encounters are classic Vietnam types--a career sergeant,
a bar girl, a flashy and heroic helicopter pilot, etc.
The sparse dialogue is ungainly, with no general conversations among groups of persons. The hero is
first given clerical duties. When he later goes into
combat, he murders a number of allied Vietnamese

servicemen. After that and other adventures, he
flies home to resume civilian life. The book does
not reach a conclusion in any customary literary
sense; it just stops.

100.   Smith, Steven Phillip. American Boys. New York:
            G. P. Putnam's Sons, 1975. 435pp. 74-16619.

The characters in this long, thoughtful novel are
Army enlisted men in an air mobile infantry unit in
the central highlands of Vietnam. The time appears
to be 1966 or 1967. Four men transfer to Vietnam
from Germany and serve as riflemen and helicopter
door gunners. There is much combat action, and the
book offers a full picture of helicopter warfare in
support of infantry. The men suffer variously. One,
a former football star, begins to murder prisoners.
He is later badly wounded. Another man is killed,
and the two survivors struggle with fatalism, narcotics, and alcoholism. At the end of the novel, only
one of the four boards the airplane to return home.
In contrast to many accounts of Vietnam, the soldiers
here are professionally competent and proud of their
ability to fight. There are, however, the usual conflicts between low-ranking enlisted men and professional officers and NCOs.

101.   Sparrow, Gerald. Java Weed. London: Triton Books,
            1968. 160pp.

The narrator of this short first-person novel is a
British newspaper reporter in Vietnam. With two
colleagues, an American and a Eurasian woman, he
is captured by the Vietcong and taken to a jungle
prison camp, where conditions include debasement
and torture. The reporters escape and hide in float-
ing clumps of Java weed in the Mekong River. After
many adventures, and with help from friendly Vietnamese, they finally reach freedom. The prison-
camp sequences are unpleasant, but like the entire
novel, they lack convincing detail.

102.   Stone, Robert. Dog Soldiers. Boston: Houghton

Mifflin Company, 1973.   342pp.   74-11441.
New York: Ballantine Books, 1975.

This story of the illegal narcotics trade is set for
the most part in California, but the initial chapters
describe action in Vietnam.   Many of the characters
are either military veterans or civilians associated
in some capacity with the war effort.   They are accordingly somewhat brutalized, embittered, and fully
familiar with small arms and individual tactics.   The
book points out the corruption in Vietnam that facil-
itated the narcotics trade during the war.   It is a
credible story that provides the basis for the motion
picture Who'll Stop the Rain?

103.   Stone, Scott C. S.   The Coasts of War.   New York:
         Pyramid, 1966.   157pp.

In addition to being one of the few Navy novels of
Vietnam, this excellent little book is also one of the
earliest, apparently set in 1964.   One of the principal
events, for instance, is the first combat air strike
by U.S. Navy jets in Vietnam.   The story has to do
with Lt. Eriksen, a Navy officer advising a Vietnamese small-boat patrol force in the Mekong Delta.
Eriksen is a competent and enthusiastic professional
officer, and the Vietnamese he advises are capable
patriots.   In keeping with this positive tone, they are
usually successful in military and even political action
against the Vietcong.   This is not, however, a foolish
book.   The characters and situations are believable,
and the writing is able.

104.   Tauber, Peter.   The Last Best Hope.   New York:
         Harcourt Brace Jovanovich, 1977.   628pp.   76-
         0730.

This huge book is clearly intended to be a statement
about the generation of Americans that reached ma-
turity during the 1960s.   Indeed, many of the characters are recognizable as prosperous, well-educated,
verbose young people who made themselves and what
passed for their ideas apparent in that unfortunate
decade.   One of them is drafted and sent to Vietnam.

Scenes of the war cover a substantial number of pages.
Willie Bowen, the soldier, is an Army enlisted man,
although his location and military assignment are
neither clear nor consistent. During one adventure,
he survives a battle and hides for a while in a friendly
village. Later, he leads a patrol to save a general
officer whose helicopter has been shot down. For that
achievement, he is awarded the Congressional Medal
of Honor by a newly elected Richard Nixon.

105.   Taylor, Thomas. A-18. New York: Crown Publish-
            ers, Inc., 1967. 273pp. 67-26244.

Taylor, an Army officer and Vietnam veteran, offers
the rather fanciful tale of a Special Forces team sent
to North Vietnam to kill or capture two important politicians. The greater part of the book has to do with
the background, selection, and training of the team.
This takes place in Hawaii, Okinawa, and Formosa.
The characters are professional, long-service soldiers.
They and their dialogue seem sometimes to belong in
World War II, but they make quite a contrast to the
unmotivated draftees who populate so many Vietnam
novels. The mission into North Vietnam occupies
only the last thirty or so pages, and it is described
in a relatively spare and hurried manner when compared with the earlier and very full accounts of Special Forces procedures, equipment, and training.
What is most apparent throughout is Taylor's sincere
admiration of the Special Forces.

106.   Taylor, Thomas. A Piece of This Country. New
            York: W. W. Norton & Company, Inc., 1970.
            192pp. 70-105739.

The central problem with this story is that Taylor,
a white officer, is writing about a black main character, Jackson, an NCO. From the advantageous
perspective of a decade after the book was published,
it is reasonable to guess that many blacks would find
the character of Jackson patronizing. The plot centers on the defense of a small Vietnamese outpost
near the Laotian border in 1965. Jackson, an out-
standing soldier, is induced to extend his stay in

Vietnam and to replace a deceased captain as senior
adviser to the Vietnamese garrison. Jackson deals
with the military and personnel situation at the camp
and effects an improvement in its fighting potential.
The difference in outlook between American and Vietnamese soldiers is presented with convincing force.
Also, scenes of combat are fast-paced and expert.
In the end, Jackson emerges as a sort of hero, but
Taylor conveys the impression that the North Vietnamese and Vietcong will be the final victors.

107.   Tiede, Tom. Coward. New York: Trident Press,
            1968. 383pp. 68-18311.

Tiede expresses the tragedy and injustice of the Vietnam War with effectiveness. His main character is
Nathan Long, an Army private who begins a hunger
strike at his post in the United States to avoid going
to Vietnam. He is unsure of the rightness of the war,
but principally he is afraid and he admits it. Long
is court-martialed and assigned as a company clerk
to an infantry unit somewhere near Saigon. The time
seems to be the mid- or late 1960s. The Vietnamese
and their country are truly revolting to the young man,
who is simply terrified of the war. After his friend
is killed, Long volunteers for a patrol that ends in
his capture, torture, and death. The few scenes of
combat are not as effective as those set in military
rear areas.

108.   Trowbridge, James. Easy Victories. Boston:
            Houghton Mifflin Company, 1973. 214pp. 72-
            9018.

Knox, an American intelligence agent, is both amoral
and lucky. Assigned to Vietnam prior to the 1968
Tet offensive, he talks his way out of a dangerous
posting in the field and arranges instead to do relatively safe work in Saigon. Among the rear-area
military men, war profiteers, bar girls, and civilians,
Knox manages to find a place and to enjoy himself.
He acquires a mistress and begins to make money in
illegal currency manipulations. The impression conveyed is that intelligence officers and indeed most

other people in Saigon are fools, traitors, alcoholics,
or worse. Finally, Knox is nearly killed during Tet,
his mistress kills herself, and he decides it is time
to get out. Lucky until the end, Knox manages to
break his contract with the intelligence service and
find a first-class seat on a plane back to the United
States.

109.   Tully, Andrew. The Time of the Hawk. New York:
            William Morrow & Company, Inc., 1967.
            335pp. 67-11637.

Set at a time in the near future, this early novel
describes a Vietnam much as it may actually have
been in the early 1950s. A cease-fire has ended
the fighting, but American troops still occupy the
country as a bewildering array of political individuals and factions seek to control the government
of Vietnam. The forces of Peking are a particularly
sinister and strong element. Order is brought out
of this chaos by U.S. Senator Baldwin, who secretly
represents a hawkish American President. The middle-
aged, sedentary senator performs activities that would
tax the abilities of a soldier, athlete, spy, and youth-
ful lover. Despite the implausibility of its parts, the
whole book comes together as a coherent story.

110.   Vaughn, Robert. The Valkyrie Mandate. New York:
            Simon and Schuster, 1974. 287pp. 73-16880.

Into the background of the coup that will overthrow
the Diem government, the author inserts fictional
characters and events. Lt. Colonel Justin Barclay
is an able military adviser with years of experience
in Vietnam and the unusual ability to speak and understand the language. Barclay is ordered to offer American aid to one group of plotting Vietnamese officers,
but he decides on his own initiative to deal with another group instead. Barclay picks his conspirators
well, and the coup is successful. However, the end,
among convolutions of Vietnamese politics, is not to
the planned advantage of any of the Americans involved.

111.   Vaughn, Robert, and Monroe Lynch. Brandywine's
       War. np: Bartholomew House, Ltd., 1971.
       249pp. 77-155027.

By manipulating the essential stupidity of all wars,
the authors manage to write a funny book about Vietnam. Chief Warrant Officer W. W. Brandywine
is a recovery-and-supply officer in a helicopter unit
where everyone, it seems, is either a fool or a
scoundrel. Brandywine is skilled at finding supplies
and equipment through all sorts of means, and he is
also an adept practical joker. The unit is commanded
by a publicity-seeking general whose life is run by a
PFC, the self-proclaimed son of the Secretary of Defense. Amid the humor generated by such characters,
men occasionally fight and die in the real war. These
scenes of combat and death appear as rather abrupt
surprises in the text. Unlike most Vietnam novels,
this one begins and ends with almost all of the principal characters still in place.

112.   Webb, James. Fields of Fire. Englewood Cliffs,
       New Jersey: Prentice-Hall, Inc., 1978. 344pp.
       78-4046. New York: Bantam, 1979.

This painful and realistic account of a Marine infantry
platoon near An Hoa in 1968 is one of the best novels
of the Vietnam War. Webb effectively conveys the experiences, attitudes, and relationships of Marine enlisted men and junior officers. The dialogue rings
true and accurate. The enemies in numerous small-
unit actions are both Vietcong and North Vietnamese
regulars. Neither force is elusive; both are very
much in evidence, and the Marines fight them with
competence and professional skill. There are the
usual hostilities between junior enlisted men and the
professional soldiers who command them. Ugly racial hatred is more apparent in base camp than in
the field. Death, however, is color blind, and by
the end of the book, many of the characters are dead
and others are badly wounded. This is not a pretty
story, but it is an excellent novel.

113.   Williams, Alan. The Tale of the Lazy Dog.
       London: Anthony Bland, 1970. 287pp.

Murray, an Irish writer and old hand in Southeast
Asia, learns of occasional shipments of large amounts
of American currency from Tan Son Hut airbase back
to the United States. With the help of numerous persons from many countries in Southeast Asia, he arranges a plan to steal one of the shipments. Among
his assistants is the Algerian-French wife of an American CIA official, and part of the plot involves a staged
Vietcong attack on the airbase, so credibility is not
high. There are several rather offhand murders, as
the conspirators simply kill everyone who gets in
their way. The crime is successful, but the writer
and his colleagues soon find themselves and their loot
in the hands of the North Vietnamese, who had been
the secret sponsors of the plan all along.

114.   Williams, John A. _Captain Blackman._ Garden City,
            New York: Doubleday & Company, Inc., 1972.
            336pp. 75-171328.

Abraham Blackman serves as the typical black American soldier from the Revolution through Vietnam,
where he is the Captain Blackman of the title. Vietnam scenes are a relatively small part of the book,
but they touch upon the growing role of blacks in the
Army and upon the racial tension that was certainly
a fact of life in the Army in the 1960s. Throughout
the book, in all historical eras, Blackman must con-
tinually fight the racial prejudice of the Army establishment. A tendency to see all things black as good
and all things white as evil hurts the credibility of
an otherwise effective story.

115.   Wilson, William. _The LBJ Brigade._ Los Angeles:
            Apocalypse, 1966. 124pp. 65-28536. Los
            Angeles: Parallax, 1966. New York: Pyramid
            Books, 1966.

For such an early book, the antiwar message here is
overwhelming. The narrator, who is not named, tells
of his service as an Army infantryman in the present
tense. Settings and actions are simplified. Upon ar-
riving in Vietnam, the hero meets Sace, an experienced sergeant who tries to teach him how to stay

alive. However, he disobeys the sergeant's instruc-
tions and as a result Sace is killed and he is captured by the Vietcong. After some time observing
the superior tactics of the enemy, the narrator is
killed in an air strike.

116.   Wolfe, Michael. The Two-Star Pigeon. New York:
       Harper & Row, 1975. 244pp. 74-5804.

This fascinating but implausible story has to do with
an attempt to restore the Vietnamese monarchy in the
person of a child emperor. Much of the action takes
place in Dalat, and there are full descriptions of that
town and of the Vietnamese military academy located
there. Among the would-be monarchists are an American major general and various Vietnamese soldiers
and politicans. Their goals are to unify the country
against the North Vietnamese and to secure benefits
for themselves. An unqualified but inspired Army
intelligence agent foils the plot by kidnapping the
proposed emperor, and it develops that the child is
an impostor without imperial lineage. These events
occur after 1968 but at a time when Americans are
still fully in charge of the war.

117. Chung, Ly Qui (ed.). Between Two Fires. New
York: Praeger Publishers, 1970. 119pp. 72-
126776.

Four of the nine stories in this collection have American characters or relate in some substantial way to
Americans.

117a. Bi, Nguyen Tan. "When the Americans Came." pp.
3-14.

A two-month stay of an American company in a
Vietnamese village is viewed from the perspective of the villagers. They are able to see
little difference between the Americans and the
French. Little is gained militarily, and the life
of the village is disrupted.

117b. Chau, Thanh. "The Tears of Tan Qui Dong." pp. 21-
41.

A resettlement village near Saigon is the scene of
fighting in May of 1968. A family is forced to
evacuate. They observe American tanks and helicopters in combat against the enemy. From incidental fire, the villagers suffer material and human
losses.

117c. Thao, Chu. "Resuscitation of the Dead Earth." pp. 53-
61.

In the small village of Binh Hoa, near Highway 1,

an American unit is attacked by the Vietcong. In
addition to more customary reactions, the Americans later defoliate the area. Afterward, local
farmers find that nothing will grow in the soil.
Finally, they import earthworms, and the soil begins to live again.

117d   Nguyen, Pham Ngoc. "House for Rent." pp. 63-
        73.

        In 1969, a Vietnamese soldier searches for housing
        for his family in Danang. He finds that the city has
        been economically and socially harmed by the Amer-
        icans, and he is unable to afford decent housing on
        his soldier's pay.

118.   Karlin, Wayne, Basil T. Paquet, and Larry Rottman,
        (eds.). Free Fire Zone. Coventry, Connecticut:
        1st Casualty Press, 1973. 208pp. 72-12486.
        New York: McGraw-Hill Book Company, 1973.

        This is the most complete and best-edited collection
        of Vietnam short stories.

118a.   McCusker, Michael Paul. "The Old Man." pp. 1-2.

        An American infantryman, on a sweep through a
        village, kills an old man for amusement. After-
        ward, he feels nothing.

118b.   Pelfrey, William. "Bangalore." pp. 3-12.

        A new replacement in an Army unit is sent to join
        more experienced men at an ambush site. With
        careful planning and technique, the men success-
        fully attack and kill five Vietcong.

118c.   Grajewsky, Julian. "The Meeting." pp. 14-16.

        A soldier awakes in the morning and walks from
        his bunker down to a nearby river to bathe. A

leopard with bloody paws and mouth drinks from
the opposite bank.

118d. Karlin, Wayne. "Medical Evacuation." pp. 17-19.

A helicopter door gunner flies into the field for
a medical evacuation. At the landing site, he
fires at suspected enemy positions. After the
ship returns to base, the wounded and dead are
removed.

118e. Dorris, James R. "The Accident." pp. 21-27.

Temple, a sergeant, and Adams, a major, are
assigned to a support unit near Bien Hoa. They
take a jeep to a Vietnamese army compound for a
meeting. On the return trip, while Adams is
driving, they accidentally hit and kill an old man.
Over Adams's objections, Temple insists on tell-
ing their commanding officer, a colonel. The colonel explains that the matter is not important enough
to ruin the career of a good officer, and it is
forgotten.

118f. Smith, Steve. "First Light." pp. 28-39.

After he kills civilians during a mistaken attack on
a village, a helicopter door gunner is harassed by
a rear-area sergeant. He attempts to kill the
sergeant, but he is brought under control by a
friend.

118g. Little, Loyd. "Out with the Lions." pp. 41-50.

Two Special Forces troopers lead a party of Nung
mercenaries to an outpost on the Cambodian border.
On the way back, they are ambushed. After taking
minor wounds, they learn from shouting that their
attackers are Nungs in the employ of the Vietcong.
An arrangement is made to end the battle, and each
party goes its separate way.

118h. Karlin, Wayne. "Search and Destroy." pp. 51-54.

Marine helicopter crewmen share quarters that are
infested with rats. After several unsuccessful attempts, they manage to kill a mother and ten bab-
ies.

118i. Karlin, Wayne. "The Vietnamese Elections." pp. 56-
58.

Marine helicopter crewmen are ordered to kill two
of their three pet dogs. They conduct an election
to make the choice and kill the two losers.

118j. Huddle, David. "The Interrogation of Prisoner Bung
by Mr. Hawkins and Sergeant Tree." pp. 59-
67. Also in his A Dream with No Stump Roots
in It. np: University of Missouri Press, 1975.
74-22229. pp. 17-26; and in Esquire, 75, 1
(January 1971), 128-129, 156, 158, 160, 162.

An American and a Vietnamese interrogate a Vietcong suspect. After they beat him and he supplies
some information, they release him. The prisoner
returns to his village happy that he has been able
to gather so much information for his Vietcong unit
at the cost of only a minor beating.

118k. Kimpel, John M. "And Even Beautiful Hands Cry."
pp. 69-79.

A soldier living in Saigon falls in love with a Vietnamese bar girl. When her friend's child becomes
ill, the soldier arranges for it to be treated in an
American hospital. The baby dies, and from this,
somehow, the love affair is broken.

118l. Aitken, James. "Lederer's Legacy." pp. 80-96.

Lederer and his buddies work in a unit whose job
it is to write commendations. His legacy is a list
of phrases in specialized military terminology de-

scribing the heroism or futility of men who show
bravery in combat.

118m. Bobrowsky, Igor. "The Courier." pp. 98-107.

A Marine infantryman attempts to organize and
control his thoughts as he drives a jeep in a con-
voy. He remembers the death and fear of battles.

118n. Shields, James. "The Candidate." pp. 108-117.
Also in Caroline Quarterly (Spring 1972).

Mixed together in this particularly difficult story
are reflections about racial tension in the military
and observations about railroad tracks in the jungle
in Vietnam.

118o. Rottmann, Larry. "Thi Bong Dzu." pp. 119-125.

Thi Bong Dzu is an adolescent rice farmer in a
village north of Saigon. On the eve of his twelfth
birthday, he sets out to assist his Vietcong squad
and is killed in an ambush.

118p. Pitts, Oran R. "Temporary Duty." pp. 126-134.

Three enlisted men from a medical support unit are
sent forward to an evacuation hospital for thirty
days. They find the situation there quite frighten-
ing, and the experience helps them put their previ-
ous problems into better perspective.

118q. Karlin, Wayne. "R & R." pp. 136-143.

During the Tet holiday in 1967, a Marine spends a
brief recreation leave in Saigon. He goes through
the usual experiences with bars, girls, and American food, but he finds the leave unsatisfying.

118r. Davis, George. "Ben." pp. 144-146.

A black lieutenant is offered a teenage Vietnamese
girl by her parents. Although he is not interested
in having sex, he takes the girl for a walk as he
thinks about the war and his part in it.

118s. Tavela, John. "The Souvenir." pp. 148-153.

A middle-aged overweight mess sergeant falls in
love with a Vietnamese woman. He offers her
various gifts and promises to take her to America
with him. She agrees, but later he learns that she
has been trading sex to another soldier for his
promise, too, to take her to America.

118t. Paquet, Basil T. "Warren." pp. 154-175.

Warren is an enlisted man working with the living
and dead at a hospital near Bien Hoa. His work
and recreation seem to be depressing and pointless.
There are explicit accounts of his relationships with
prostitutes.

118u. Karlin, Wayne. "Extract." pp. 177-182.

Joshua, a door gunner on a helicopter, goes on a
mission to extract a group of reconnaissance Marines in the Demilitarized Zone. He appears to
be only mildly interested in what he is doing.

118v. Davis, George. "Ben." pp. 183-186.

Ben Williams, a black pilot, is on leave in Bang-
kok. In a bar, he meets a black soldier who is
AWOL and plans to escape to Sweden. Ben sym-
pathizes with the man.

118w. Currer, Barry. "The Rabbi." pp. 188-201.

The Rabbi is the nickname of Lt. Rowan, who commands a military police detachment in Saigon. Rowan knows the city and the language well; he is

happy in his job and has extended his tour several
times. Unfortunately, one of his subordinates makes
a mistake, and the threat of an investigation forces
Rowan to leave for the United States.

118x. Mueller, Quentin. "Children Sleeping--Bombs Falling."
pp. 202-204.
An American walks among the children of Danang,
gathering last impressions of Vietnam on the day
before he leaves for Okinawa.

119. Klinkowitz, Jerome, and John Somer (eds.). Writing
Under Fire. New York: Delta, 1978. 274pp.
78-17682.

This collection includes nonfiction and critical pieces
as well as stories that are not set recognizably in
Vietnam. Those stories that fit the scope of this bibliography are annotated below.

119a. Kaplan, Johanna. "Dragon Lady." pp. 22-34. Also
in Harper's Magazine, 241, 1442 (July 1970),
78-83.

A Chinese girl, brought up in Cholon, becomes a
Vietcong assassin. Her specialty, until she is
caught, is shooting Americans and Vietnamese from
the back of a motorcycle. She uses a .45 pistol.

119b. Porche, Don. "Evenings in Europe and Asia." pp.
35-42. Also in Prairie Schooner, 46, 2 (Summer 1972), 96-104.

On a visit to Europe, a young man develops and
expresses his reservations about war and killing.
Later, he compromises in order to serve as a
radio operator in Vietnam.

119c. Mayer, Tom. "A Birth in the Delta." pp. 43-57.
Also in his The Weary Falcon (see entry 120c).

119d. Eastlake, William. "The Biggest Thing Since Custer."
       pp. 58-68. Also in Atlantic Monthly, 222,
       3 (September 1978), 92-97.

       An infantry company is wiped out in northern Viet-
       nam. The event is compared to the massacre of
       Custer's troops at the Battle of the Little Big Horn,
       as photographers and graves registration personnel
       process the bodies.

119e. Kolpacoff, Victor. "The Room." pp. 71-89. Also
       in New American Review, n. 1 (1967) pp. 7-27.

       A former officer, now a prisoner, is forced to
       assist in the interrogation of a Vietcong suspect.
       The room in which the interrogation takes place is
       described in detail.

119f. Parker, Thomas. "Troop Withdrawal--The Initial Step."
       pp. 90-107. Also in Harper's Magazine, 239,
       1431 (August 1969), 61-78; and in Gulassa, Cyril
       M. (ed.). The Fact of Fiction. San Francisco:
       Canfield Press, 1972. 75-184742. pp. 67-85.

       In 1968, a specialist fourth-class and a lieutenant
       who are longtime adversaries, work in an Army
       hospital near Saigon. Through able and astute use
       of military forms and regulations, the specialist
       manages to have the lieutenant declared officially
       dead.

119g. Major, Clarence. "Dossy O." pp. 108-110. Also
       in Black Creation, 3, 4 (Summer 1972), 4-5.

       This story has to do with the attitudes and percep-
       tions of black soldiers serving in Vietnam. The
       language, a sort of black slang, is particularly dif-
       ficult to follow.

119h. Baber, Asa. "The Ambush." pp. 130-135. Also
       in The Falcon, 4, 4 (Spring 1972), 39-44; and
       with the title "Ambush: Laos, 1960," in TRI-

QUARTERLY, 45 (Spring 1979), 165-171 (see
entry 122b).

119i. West, Thomas A. , Jr. "Gone Are the Men." pp.
136-145. Also in Transatlantic Review, 41
(Winter-Spring 1972), 35-45.

This awkward story seems to be made up of the
thoughts of a soldier during either an artillery attack or a religious service. Among his reflections
are poems and the lyrics to songs.

119j. Woods, W. C. "He That Died of Wednesday." pp.
152-164. Also in Esquire, 6 (June 1969), 213-
217.

This touching story includes a brief description of
events in the war, but it deals mostly with the re-
conciliation of a returning soldier with his girlfriend.
She had been unfaithful to him and had donated
money and blood to the enemy, but they still love
each other and plan to be married.

119k. Chatain, Robert. "On the Perimeter." pp. 209-226.
Also in New American Review, 13 (1971), 112-
131.

An Army enlisted man reflects on many aspects of
the war as he stands guard on the perimeter. His
numerous thoughts are all rather brief and they
change quickly.

120. Mayer, Tom. The Weary Falcon. Boston: Houghton
Mifflin Company, 1971. 174pp. 75-132335.

120a. "The Weary Falcon." pp. 1-54.

Chaney is a warrant officer flying a Cobra helicopter out of An Khe. He flies with Slade, a regular
Army captain, and with Mood, a new pilot. In an
active day, which is quite revealing of the helicopter

war, both Slade and Mood are killed. Chaney visits
each of their rooms afterward and comes to know
more about them. At the end of the story, he is
even more weary than at the beginning.

120b. "A Walk in the Rain." pp. 55-57.

An inexperienced Special Forces officer leads a patrol of Vietnamese over the border into Laos. They
engage in minor and inconclusive action. The officer does his job well, but he is not sure whether
he has the courage and ability for real combat.
Back at his base, he learns that another patrol was
attacked and that an American was wounded. Then
he is told that he will take out another patrol soon.

120c. "The Last Operation." pp. 79-110. Also in Playboy,
       14 (August 1967), 97, 131-134, 136-137, with the
       title, "Anson's Last Assignment" (see entry 162).

Bender, an American photojournalist, and Anson, an
English photographer, visit a Korean Unit. The
Koreans are sharp, capable, and well-motivated
troops. The visitors observe karate practice and
fly to a company in the field that has just been in
combat. Anson is killed just before he intended to
return to England.

120d. "Kafka for President." pp. 111-147.

Bender, an American reporter, visits a Marine
Combined Action Company outside of Danang. The
company assists with civic and defense projects in
a village. On one patrol with the Marines, Bender
witnesses the capture and later the torture of a
female Vietcong. Under pressure, she reveals that
the Vietnamese girlfriend of one of the Marines is
also a Vietcong. The two women are later taken
away.

120e. "A Birth in the Delta." pp. 149-174. Also in Klin-
       kowitz, Jerome, and John Somer (eds.). Writing
       Under Fire (see entry 119c).

An Army company in the Mekong Delta engages and destroys a Vietcong encampment. Among the ruined huts, they find a dead woman with a live baby at the point of being born. The company medic performs a crude operation in an attempt to save the baby, but he is unsuccessful, and the child dies.

121. Suddick, Tom. A Few Good Men. Samisdat, 4, 1
      (1974). 116pp.

In his introduction to this entire issue of Samisdat, Suddick suggests that the work may be considered a story collection or a novel. After reading, the former seems more reasonable. Like most Samisdat issues seen for this bibliography, the reproduction is of poor quality. The characters are Marines in the early 1970s.

121a. "Caduceus." pp. 8-21.

A Navy corpsman attached to a Marine infantry unit deals with the squalor of life in a bunker as well as with his professional duties. At one point, he kills a man too badly wounded to survive.

121b. "A Hotel on Park Place." pp. 21-35.

A staff sergeant in a rear area is a capable hustler and promoter. Among other things, he is a consistent winner of Monopoly games. He arranges to assume the management of a large post exchange and to have a suspicious Vietnamese medical officer killed.

121c. "If a Frog Had Wings." pp. 35-45.

Two enlisted Marines take a rest and recuperation leave in Taiwan because Australia and other more desirable places are not available. During the leave, they devote their time to alcohol and sex, but they cannot forget the war.

121d. "It Was A Great Fight, Ma." pp. 46-66.

A lance corporal, new to Vietnam, is assigned as
a radioman. Before he can fully learn his trade,
most of his company is captured. He and a few
other survivors are assigned to another unit.

121e. "A Shithouse Rat." pp. 69-78. Also in Samisdat, 2,
2 & 3 (Summer-Fall 1974), 25-36.

A group of enlisted men is assigned to burn human
waste. They steal the private files of a senior
NCO and throw them into the burning pit. As the
NCO orders them to dig the files out with their
hands, a rocket attack kills him.

121f. "Totenkopf." pp. 79-89.

After returning from Vietnam, a former Marine con-
tinues his business of selling war souvenirs, including human skulls. Once, he uses the skull of a
dead Marine, and that man's brother seeks him out
and tries to kill him. Instead, the salesman be-
heads the brother and plans to sell his skull, too.

121g. "The Two Hundreth Eye." pp. 89-107.

A lieutenant in a psychiatric hospital believes his
eye is missing as the result of capture and torture
by the enemy. The scenes which the lieutenant
remembers are quite realistic and horrible.

121h. "The Diehard." pp. 108-116. Also in The Berkeley
Samisdat Review, 1, 1 (June 1973), 1-12; and in
Clifton, Merritt (ed.). The Tower Anthology of
the San Jose Movement in Fiction. San Jose,
California: np, 1974, pp. 1-7.

A lance corporal is separated from his unit, and
he survives for months, possibly for years, in the
jungle. When he is finally rescued by Vietnamese
troops, he refuses to believe that the American

troops have gone home. Sent to an American psychiatric hospital, he believes the staff are Russian
interrogators.

122. TRI-QUARTERLY, 45 (Spring 1979).

Five war stories in this special issue are set in Vietnam.

122a. Anderson, Kent. "Sympathy for the Devil." pp. 99-
150.

Sergeant Hanson and the other Special Forces NCOs
in his unit have adapted well to the war. They
treat each other with a balance of affection and offhand brutality. In their camp among Montagnards,
they fight the enemy with a frightened professional-
ism that is entirely convincing. Hanson survives,
and on the airplane home he loads a souvenir pistol so he will be comfortable.

122b. Baber, Asa. "Ambush: Laos, 1960." pp. 165-171.
Also in The Falcon, 4, 4 (Spring 1972), 39-44;
and, with the title "The Ambush," in Klinkowitz,
Jerome, and John Somer (eds.). Writing Under
Fire (see entry 119h).

A Marine officer is a patient in the hospital at
Camp Pendleton. He suffers psychological prob-
lems because of his cowardice in an ambush in
Laos, which is described briefly.

122c. Ehrhart, W. D. "I Drink My Coffee Black." pp.
172-177.

Bill Ehrhart brings the fine touch of a poet to this
tight story of a Marine in Hue in 1968. His character, an experienced infantryman, thinks about
home and many other things as he fires an occasional shot out of a window in a building where he
has taken refuge. He is also making a cup of coffee. In his preoccupation, he forgets the essential

rule of combat that one should never fire twice
from the same place, and he pays the price for his
neglect.

122d. Heinemann, Larry. "The First Clean Fact." pp.
       178-188.

This first-person account is in what seems to be
black street patois. It is a rambling account of the
experiences and attitudes of a black soldier in Vietnam. It is difficult to follow, and the surprise at
the end is that the narrator is dead, having been
killed in an air strike.

122e. Coleman, Charles A., Jr. "In Loco Parentis." pp.
       189-197.

The setting here is a military psychiatric hospital
in Texas, but a lengthy flashback explains how a
patient, Eddie Sailor, broke down in a battle and
was sent to the hospital. Most of the dialogue occurs between Eddie and a psychiatrist who is at-
tempting to prepare him for a review board that
has the power to decide his future.

123. Abbott, Lee K. "The Viet Cong Love of Sgt. Donnie
    T. Bobo." North American Review, 264, 3
    (Winter 1979), 43-47.

    Lee K. Abbott is successful at the very difficult busi-
    ness of writing a funny story about the Vietnam War.
    The narrator, Leon Busby, and his lifelong friend
    Donnie Bobo are all over Vietnam in 1967 and 1968
    practicing their specialty of coaxing Vietcong out of
    tunnels. They use the English language and such
    blandishments as Otis Redding records. A female
    Vietcong resists Bobo, but after she is captured, he
    falls in love with her and finds a Korean priest to
    marry them. Then they disappear. Back in the United
    States after the war, Busby hears from Bobo that the
    couple are happily settled in Ho Chi Minh City.

124. Algren, Nelson. "Police and Mama-sans Get It All."
    In his The Last Carousel. New York: G. P.
    Putnam's Sons, 1973. 72-97289. pp. 144-150.

    Although listed in a standard index as a short story,
    this may well be journalism. A Vietnamese prostitute
    who maintains both pride and hope despite her working
    conditions is befriended by an American. After she
    sees the relative luxury of his hotel room, she tries
    to move into his life. Although the American admires
    her spirit, he declines the proffered arrangement.

125. Algren, Nelson. "What Country Do You Think You're
    In?" In his The Last Carousel. New York:
    G. P. Putnam's Sons, 1973. 72-97289. pp.
    138-143.

71

Like the other Algren work listed here, this may be
journalism. An American civilian lives in a hotel in
Saigon in 1969. Among his acquaintances are a deaf-
mute Vietnamese prostitute and her teenage son. He
invites them to join him for dinner on a riverboat res-
tuarant. On the appointed day, the boy insists that
the American join him at a cricket fight instead. Later, the American learns that the restaurant had been
bombed that day.

126. Baber, Asa. "The French Lesson." Playboy, 28,
      3 (March 1981), 98-100, 108, 202, 205-206, 208.

The narrator is a Marine officer who has just resigned
his commission after losing three men on a clandestine
mission near the Plain of Jars in Laos. The time is
1961, and as he waits in Vientiane for orders, he
learns the identity of a Frenchman who may have been
involved in the deaths of his men. The former officer
kills the man. He is immediately returned to the U.S.,
where he is debriefed and released from the Marine
Corps.

127. Belanger, Charles A. "Once Upon a Time When It
      Was Night." In Schultz, John (ed.). Angels
      in My Oven. Chicago: Columbia College Press,
      1976. 75-33527. pp. 76-86.

An Army helicopter pilot, on his second tour in Vietnam, is in the shower at his base when a rocket attack occurs. Although he is unwilling to seem afraid,
the situation becomes serious and he joins others in a
bunker. After the attack, the men drink beer on the
roof of their quarters and discuss aspects of the war,
including their fear, their hatred of the antiwar movement in the United States, and their chances of sur-
vival.

128. Bonazzi, Robert. "Light Casualties." Transatlantic
      Review, 28 (Spring 1968), 46-51.

Specific locations are not mentioned, but this appears
to be a story of the Vietnam War. Two brothers meet

in a field hospital where one is on the staff and the
other is a wounded front-line soldier. The unwounded
man describes the meeting as he plans letters to his
mother.

129.   Brunner, John. "The Inception of the Epoch of Mrs.
        Bedonebyasyoudid." In his From This Day For-
        ward. Garden City, New York: Doubleday &
        Company, Inc., 1972. pp. 215-222.

        Although this story unfolds in a direct, linear fashion,
        the Vietnamese connection is established only at the end.
        In New York City, a group of young men of several
        races set booby traps that kill and maim numerous
        citizens. It is then revealed that they are working
        for a Vietcong officer who lives under cover in the
        city. Their next project is to be a mortar bombard-
        ment of New York.

130.   Chatain, Robert. "The Adventures of the Mantises."
        New American Review, 7 (August 1969), 150-158.
        Also in Gulassa, Cyril M. (ed.). The Fact of
        Fiction. San Francisco: Canfield Press, 1972.
        75-184742. pp. 104-111.

        A group of soldiers in a rear area near Bien Hoa feed
        insects to a mantis. Various men walk up and are
        absorbed in the action.

131.   Clifton, Merritt. "In the Field." Gar, 2, 8 (1973).

        An infantryman, probably in the Army, is assigned a
        new buddy on patrol. Having seen new men come and
        go, he is not particularly interested in this person,
        who wears a peace medallion on his neck and has two
        notches on the stock of his rifle. At the end of an
        uneventful patrol, the new man kills a peasant woman
        who seems suspicious. Passing airplanes mask the
        shot.

132.   De Grazia, Emilio. "The Sniper." Samisdat, 17, 1
        (Spring 1978), 29-42.

The narrator is an Army sniper, chosen for the job
because he had volunteered for special duty. "It re-
minded me that in the Army I could only do the things
I didn't want to do." In addition to his work, which
is described in minute detail, the sniper writes to a
girl back home, considers a scheme to buy rifles as
counterfeit souvenirs, and plans for his forthcoming
leave in New Zealand. Toward the end of the story,
he no longer shoots at available targets. Instead, he
tries only to survive. Reproduction in the review
copy of this periodical is poor, and in some places
the text is impossible to read.

133.   Deighton, Len. "First Base." In his Eleven Decla-
          rations of War. New York: Harcourt Brace
          Jovanovich, 1971. 74-13068. pp. 98-115.

Two Army truckdrivers become lost in the rain somewhere in Vietnam. After wandering for a while, they
find an abandoned American base with abundant supplies.
One of them is burned in an accident and dies shortly
afterward. The other truckdriver may still be there,
eating packaged foods and listening to popular music
recordings.

134.   Dempsey, Hank. "The Defensive Bomber." In Har-
          rison, Harry (ed.). Nova 3. New York: Walker
          and Company, 1973. 72-95775. pp. 93-111.

A North Vietnamese pilot enters the United States disguised as a student. With the help of an unsavory
group of American radicals, he obtains an aircraft and
bombs two military installations in the San Diego area.
His plan is hit and forced to land. Then he and a
black assistant are beaten to death by Americans who
reach the plane ahead of the Marines.

135.   Drake, Wayne. "The Turbulent World of Jerry Burak."
          Reed (San Jose State University), ca. 1968. pp.
          13-21.

Burak was wounded, both in mind and in body, some
years before the story occurs. He seems to have

been in Vietnam, although that place is not mentioned
specifically. He lives now with his motorcycle, a
sometime mistress, and a black friend. They smoke
a bit too much marijuana, and subsequently their house
burns down. Burak has thoughts or visions in which
the past, the present, and his imagination are mixed.
After the fire, his friend and the girl decide to move
together to Los Angeles. Burak thinks that he probably will not join them there.

136. Edelson, Morris. "A Mission in Vietnam." Quixote,
      1, 7 (June 1966), 40-43.

An Army platoon is on patrol somewhere in Vietnam
in 1966. They have just enjoyed a rest in Saigon.
The patrol encounters an old Vietnamese man with a
wagonload of personal possessions. The man sells
them some whiskey at an exorbitant price. Afterward,
when he makes an abrupt and suspicious movement,
one member of the platoon shoots and kills him. The
Americans then take the remaining alcohol and burn
the wagon and its contents. Later, when the platoon
leader reports the events to his sergeant, he is told,
"Tell your troubles to the chaplain, kid, he just went
over the hill."

137. Erhart, Stephen. "As the Hippiest Doctor Almost
         Grooved." Harper's Magazine, 242, 1452 (May
         1971), 82-84, 86.

This uncomfortable and effective story is told by a
casualty on a hospital ship off the coast of Vietnam.
At one point, the ship sails in company with the battle-
ship New Jersey, but there are no other clues as to
when the story takes place. The medical and social
routines of the ship unfold, and these seem to be the
central action of the story. There is more than enough
unpleasantness, and the touches of satire are refresh-
ingly light when compared with most Vietnam fiction.

138. Gerald, John Bart. "Walking Wounded." Harper's
         Magazine, 237, 1419 (August 1968), 45-50. Also
         in Gulassa, Cyril M. (ed.). The Fact of Fiction.

San Francisco: Canfield Press, 1972. 75-184742.
pp. 112-121.

Dunbar is an enlisted medical specialist at an Air
Force base hospital in the United States that receives
casualties from a battle zone that must be in Vietnam. Some of the wounded are in terrible physical
and psychological shape. They bring the war home
with them. Dunbar is sensitive and professionally
competent. He knows that he is fortunate not to be
in combat, and he cannot remain unaffected by his
job.

139.   Giang, Thanh, and Luu Ngo. "An American Sees the
        Light." In The Fire Blazes. Hanoi: Foreign
        Languages Publishing House, 1965. pp. 171-181.

This is the only story with an American character of
significance in a collection from North Vietnam.
Georges Fryet, an American soldier, is captured by
the Vietcong and reeducated to understand their ver-
sion of correct political and historical ideas. Finally,
after repenting his past sins, Fryet is released. The
impression is conveyed that imprisonment by the Vietcong is a sort of pleasant political summer camp.

140.   Grant, John. "Polyorfice Enterprises." Penthouse,
        January 1975, pp. 64-66, 146-148.

This strange and interesting piece of writing seems to
be part of at least two stories, and perhaps three.
One has to do with a Vietnamese prostitute; another
with a delightful old Vietnamese woman who, in effect,
buys the souls of orphans; and the third with Tex
Buchanan, a soldier who goes home to finish life in a
wheelchair. A case could be made for a theme that
ties these fragments together, but in fact they are
arranged in an awkward and surprising, but not unpleasant, manner.

141.   Grinstead, David. "A Day in Operations." Literary
        Review, 12, 1 (Autumn 1968), 103-105. Also
        in Gulassa, Cyril M. (ed.). The Fact of Fiction.

San Francisco: Canfield Press, 1972. 75-
184742. pp. 86-98.

The narrator tells his story in the present tense. He
is an experienced combat soldier who has been wounded
and assigned to assist a major in battalion operations.
The major, a veteran of World War II and Korea,
does not understand the military situation in Vietnam.
His insistence on classical military operations and
procedures regularly causes men in the field to be
killed. The narrator fails both in reasoning with the
major and in sabotaging his work, so he decides to
apply for a transfer back to his original company in
the field.

142. Haldeman, Joe. "Counterpoint." In his Infinite
       Dreams. New York: St. Martin's Press, 1978.
       78-3959. pp. 1-12.

Two men are born on the same day in 1943. Michael,
the son of a rich man, lives a life of ease and goes
to Vietnam in 1966 as an officer. Roger, the bastard
son of a New Orleans prostitute, leads a squalid life
and eventually goes to Vietnam as an enlisted artillery-
man. They do not know each other. By exercise of
bad professional judgment, Roger puts an artillery
round on Michael's position. Michael is wounded, and
the remainder of his life, through 1985, is spent as
a human vegetable in hospitals. Roger returns to
America to become a successful university professor,
but he, too, meets his final fate in a surprise ending.
This is one of the most intellectually satisfying stories
of the Vietnam War.

143.   Hannah, Barry. "Midnight and I'm Not Famous Yet."
       Esquire, 48, 500 (July 1975), 58-60, 134, 136.

An Army captain meets an old friend who is in Vietnam as an official photographer. That man joins the
captain's unit and photographs a captured enemy general. Later, the photographer is killed, and the captain kills the general as he tries to escape. After
the war, the captain is finally able to obtain a copy
of the photograph of the general from the Pentagon.

There are some unrealistic technical elements, but
this story reads well.

144. Heinemann, Larry. "Good Morning to You, Lieuten-
        ant." Harper's Magazine, 260, 1561 (June 1980),
        59-60, 64, 66-69.

This excellent story is set initially among the problems and sexual fantasies of Paco, an alcoholic Vietnam veteran in a city in the United States. Its substance, however, is a long flashback about a gang rape
in Vietnam. Paco and others who are almost certainly
Army enlisted men capture a female member of the
Vietcong. Paco remembers precisely and in detail the
physical and emotional circumstances of their subsequent rape of the captive. While they tie and rape
the woman, a lieutenant carefully ignores the event.
Finally, they kill the woman and move off. If Heinemann's purpose is to illustrate the hardening effect of
war on men's souls, he ably succeeds.

145. Ivey, Ross. "Major Little's Last Stand." Penthouse,
        11, 2 (October 1979), 144-147.

Major Little commands a helicopter unit that is based
at several places in Vietnam in 1967 and 1968. The
major has grandiose notions about war and his own
heroism. He puts his troops into a number of dangerous and stupid situations. Then he causes himself
to be awarded several medals. Subsequently, his men
capture him and tie him beneath the enlisted men's
latrine. Shortly after that, a general inspects the unit,
and Major Little is subsequently assigned to a meaning-
less job in a rear area.

146. James, Joseph. "Back in the World." Penthouse,
        6, 8 (April 1975), 65-66, 92, 94, 108.

An artillery forward observer is wounded in Vietnam.
He moves through the military hospital system back
to the United States. He then makes a rather uncomfortable adjustment to civilian life. His family and
friends want to know how it was in Vietnam. In a

Veterans' Administration Office, he observes a callous
attitude on the part of the civil servants toward veterans. A feeling is conveyed to the reader that Vietnam veterans are separated from other Americans by
differences that are almost impossible to understand
or overcome.

147. Jorgensen, Erik. "Typhoon." In Schultz, John (ed.).
      Angels in My Oven. Chicago: Columbia College
      Press, 1976. 75-33527. pp. 294-312.

      This is a fine and comprehensive story of Marine in-
      fantry at war. The time is 1968, and the narrator is
      a nineteen-year-old enlisted man. Somewhere near
      An Hoa, he and his platoon stand guard, engage in a
      firefight, murder some prisoners, walk back to base,
      endure a typhoon, and finally find a place to rest in
      camp. In this relatively short story, Jorgensen brings
      up and deals with such matters as race relations,
      personal fear, differences between career sergeants
      and privates, and other differences between rear-area
      troops and those actually engaged in combat. This is
      all done in a convincing manner, and the story moves
      at a fast pace.

148. Just, Ward. "Dietz at War." In his Honor, Power,
      Riches, Fame, and the Love of Women. New
      York: E. P. Dutton, 1979. 79-10123. pp. 73-
      86.

      Dietz is a journalist or correspondent based in an un-
      named country covering an unnamed war. The spe-
      cifics of his circumstances point unquestionably to
      Vietnam. Dietz has been there for three years. He
      has lost both his desire to return home and his jour-
      nalistic obligation to seek out and report the hard
      facts of the war. However, he has made a comfort-
      able adjustment to his environment and he intends to
      remain indefinitely.

149. Just, Ward. "Journal of a Plague Year." Atlantic
      Monthly, 232, 2 (August 1973), 87-90. Also in
      his Honor, Power, Riches, Fame, and the Love

of Women. New York: E. P. Dutton, 1979.
79-10123. pp. 87-122.

The heroine of this love story is a journalist working
in Vietnam. She moves in and out of the battle zone,
back and forth between America and Vietnam, and in
and out of a relationship with her lover, another journalist. She is certainly a stranger to most situations
and people, and her alienation may indeed be the result of exposure to the war.

150.   Just, Ward. "Prime Evening Time." In his The
        Congressman Who Loved Flaubert. Boston:
        Little, Brown and Company, 1973. 73-3189.
        pp. 93-114.

The captain in this story is not named. Having survived and won an important battle (in Vietnam?) he is
returned to the United States and awarded the Congressional Medal of Honor. He is then assigned to a
staff job in Washington, D. C. Under pressure from
his superiors, he agrees to an interview with a reporter, who asks about details of the action in which
he won the medal.

151.   Kidder, Tracy. "In Quarantine." Atlantic Monthly,
        246, 3 (September 1980), 92-100.

In this fantastic account of a homecoming from Vietnam, a lieutenant comes under the influence and control of Pancho, an enlisted man. Pancho induces him
to desert, and they find their way to a strange quarantine island. After that interlude, they board a
freighter bound for Seattle. Pancho abandons the
lieutenant, who has assumed the identity of another
officer. The lieutenant finds himself accepted by that
officer's parents into their home, and they will not
let him go.

152.   Koons, George. "Extra Man." In Schultz, John
        (ed.). Angels in My Oven. Chicago: Columbia
        College Press, 1976. 75-33527. pp. 140-144.

The narrator is the leader of a deep-penetration patrol
in Laos in 1968. The five-man squad is watching a
large group of North Vietnamese soldiers when the
extra man, a news photographer, pops a flashbulb and
reveals their position. In the ensuing attack, the
squad is nearly overrun and one man is wounded. On
a helicopter, after a successful evacuation, the narrator beats the photographer in the face with a pistol
and must be restrained from throwing him out of the
aircraft while it is in the air. Afterward, he sees the
photographer in the hospital, but they cannot communi-
cate.

153.   McDonald, Walter. "Bien Dien." Sam Houston Lit-
           erary Review, 2, 2 (November 1977), 46-53.

A group of pilots set off to take a gift of medicine to
a Vietnamese village called Bien Dien. One of them
is let off to fish in a nearby stream. At the village,
the others learn that a schoolyard was attacked by
what the Vietnamese believe were American rockets.
The Vietnamese are furious. The pilots believe the
attack was made by Vietcong mortars. They leave
and on the way back they pick up the fisherman, who
has had an uneventful day.

154.   McDonald, Walter. "Lebowitz." RE: Artes Liber-
           ales, 3, 1, (Fall 1976), 75-80.

Lebowitz, a pilot, believes he may have accidentally
attacked a Vietnamese schoolyard. In despair, he
later drops his bombs deliberately on an empty field.
This begins a feud between Lebowitz and his naviga-
tor that ultimately causes serious problems.

155.   McDonald, Walter. "New Guy." In White, James P.
           (ed.). New and Experimental Literature. Mid-
           land: Texas Center for Writers Press, 1975.
           pp. 43-50.

An Air Force officer is sent to Vietnam on temporary
duty near the end of the war. He lives through a

rocket attack on his base and wonders how anyone
can stand the war for very long.

156.   McDonald, Walter. "The Sendoff." In White, James
       P. (ed.). The Bicentennial Collection of Texas
       Short Stories. Midland: Texas Center for
       Writers Press, 1974. 78-81546. pp. 74-80.

       Eddie, an Air Force enlisted man, is on his way to
       Vietnam late in the war. On the airplane to San
       Francisco, he meets a civilian with experience in
       Vietnam who entertains him with horror stories about
       the war.

157.   McDonald, Walter. "Snow Job." Quartet, 7, 51-53,
       (Summer-Fall-Winter 1975-76), 75-84.

       An Air Force officer is on temporary duty in Vietnam
       late in the war. He is to write a history of the war.
       While a passenger on an operational Phantom flight,
       he assists in the defense of a Special Forces camp,
       and then the plane attempts but fails to save the sur-
       vivor of a radar station that has been overrun. The
       officer has an interesting and impressive reaction to
       his first experience of air combat.

158.   McDonald, Walter. "The Track." Sam Houston Lit-
       erary Review, 1, 1 (April 1976), 45-48.

       Two officers are running on an athletic track at their
       base in Vietnam. Moose is newly arrived, and Leb-
       owitz is an old hand. It is late in the war, and every-
       one is just trying to stay alive until the end.

159.   McDonald, Walter. "Waiting for the End." Descant,
       20, 4 (Summer 1976), 2-10.

       A pilot is shot down somewhere in Vietnam. He spends
       a harrowing and dangerous time on the ground, wounded,
       before being rescued. He is evacuated to a hospital,
       where he meets a wounded friend. Then he is sent
       on to Japan on a medical plane. He carries graphic
       memories of combat.

160. McNamara, Brian W. "Dust." Assay, 29, 2 (Winter
      1974), 27-28.

      A patrol, led by a lieutenant, takes a break in the
      hill country in Vietnam. Below them is a Montagnard
      village. They fear that they may have been seen by
      the enemy and that they may be subjected to mortar
      or artillery attack. In a desultory fashion, they dis-
      cuss the relative merits of fighting in the jungle versus
      fighting in the hills. After a while, they move off.

161. McNamara, Brian W. "Swanson." Assay, 29, 2
      (Winter 1974), 5-7.

      Swanson is nineteen years old and he is dying in the
      rain somewhere in Vietnam. Walking point on patrol,
      he has stepped on a mine and he is fatally injured.
      As members of his squad wait for an evacuation heli-
      copter, each of them thinks of the implications of
      Swanson's death. The squad leader thinks how it will
      affect his command; another man wants Swanson's food;
      and the squad medic thinks how futile are his attempts
      to keep Swanson alive. The story ends as the heli-
      copter arrives.

162. Mayer, Tom. "Anson's Last Assignment." Playboy,
      14 (August 1967), 97, 131-134, 136-137. Also
      in his The Weary Falcon, as "The Last Opera-
      tion" (see entry 120c).

163. O'Brien, Tim. "The Ghost Soldiers." Esquire, 95,
      3 (March 1981), 90-100.

      A particularly frightening aspect of the Vietnam War
      is evoked in this story of Army enlisted men turned
      against one another for revenge. The narrator, Herb,
      had nearly died because a medic, Jorgenson, had been
      too afraid to come to him in combat and treat him for
      a wound. Later, Herb and a friend attempt to scare
      Jorgenson to death, but Jorgenson reacts to the situ-
      ation with maturity and military professionalism. The
      game of fright, however, has become more important
      to its players than the reason that gave it birth. In

the end, Herb and Jorgenson, former enemies, are
allied in a new plan to terrify or kill another man.

164. O'Brien, Tim. "Keeping Watch by Night." Redbook,
          148, 2 (December 1976), 65-68.

A group of soldiers establish an ambush site along a
trail. As they organize themselves and their weapons,
one of them relates an act of Christian faith he wit-
nessed in Africa.

165. O'Brien, Tim. "Landing Zone Bravo." Denver Quar-
          terly, 4, 3 (August 1975), 72-77.

American infantrymen fly into an assault in a helicopter. The door gunners fire incessantly. As the aircraft takes ground fire, one man freezes. Later, he
must be forced out. As he wanders aimlessly in a
rice paddy, the door gunners shoot at him. He returns
their fire as the helicopter flies away.

166. O'Brien, Tim. "Speaking of Courage." Massachu-
          setts Review, 17, 2 (Summer 1976), 243-253.

After returning from the war, a veteran drives aimlessly around a lake in his Midwestern home town.
His uniform with its medals hangs in the closet at
home. He knows many war stories, which nobody
wants to hear.

167. O'Brien, Tim. "The Way It Mostly Was." Shenan-
          doah, 27, 2 (Winter 1976), 35-45.

A group of fifty-nine soldiers, perhaps a very depleted
company, march toward a battle in the mountains.
The unit commander, a captain, and one of the soldiers reflect independently on the nature of the war
and their parts in it. Despite differences in rank and
perspective, they reach the similar conclusion that
there is no central idea motivating the American
forces.

168. O'Brien, Tim. "Where Have You Gone, Charming
        Billy?" Redbook, 145, 1 (May 1975), 81, 127-
        132. Also in Abrahams, William. Prize Stor-
        ies 1976. Garden City, New York: Doubleday
        & Company, Inc. , 1976. pp. 211-219, under the
        title "Night March."

An Army private first-class is on a patrol. He remembers the recent death of a friend. The man had
lost a foot to a mine and then died of a heart attack.
The surviving PFC is oppressed by the war, not very
good at his job, and terrified.

169. Perea, Robert L. "Dragon Mountain." De Colores, 4,
        1 & 2 (1978), 33-41.

At a remote radio relay station, one of two American
enlisted men mistakenly shoots two ARVN soldiers.
Then he vanishes. The remaining American and a loyal
Vietnamese sergeant negotiate with the other Vietnamese soldiers and agree to pay an indemnity as ransom
for the incident. Perea writes well, and his characters are believable.

170. Perea, Robert L. "Small Arms Fire." In Anaya,
        Rudolfo A. , and Antonio Marquez (eds.). Cuentos
        Chicanos. Albuquerque, New Mexico: New
        America, 1980. pp. 43-47.

At the time of the invasion of Cambodia, two American
enlisted men come upon an ARVN truck that has hit a
mine. They call a helicopter to assist with the wounded,
but the officer in the aircraft refuses to help because
he has an important meeting. Later, the men hear
that the officer was killed by small-arms fire while
assisting another ARVN group.

171. Perea, Robert L. "A War Story." Thunderbird, 23,
        2 (December 1973), 24-25.

In the review copy, the proximity of this story to an
apparently unrelated photograph and its abrupt end at

the bottom of a page suggest that it may not be complete. As it stands, a party of Army enlisted men
visit a whorehouse in Pleiku, where they escape de-
tection by military police during a raid.

172. Pfundstein, Roy. "An Odd Coin." Ball State Univer-
        sity Forum, 13, 2 (Spring 1972), 52-56.

John, a Vietnam veteran, is insane, seemingly driven
so by the war. One of his two selves narrates the
story. He remembers scenes of dead bodies, helicopters, and his work as a sniper. He is in jail,
apparently having used his military skills to ambush
his mother when she harassed him too much after his
return from Vietnam.

173. Phong, Dinh. "A Surgical Operation." South Vietnam:
        Giai Phong Publishing House, 1969. 22pp.

This product of the National Liberation Front of South
Vietnam is dedicated "to american [sic] friends who
are struggling against the unjust war in VietNam."
The story has to do with the staff of an underground
Vietcong hospital that is faced with a wounded American soldier. In dialogue that is measured in para-
graphs, they seek a correct political solution. Although many of their family and friends have been
killed or maimed by Americans, the staff eventually
reaches the correct consensus, and an operation is
performed to save the man. Members of the hospital
staff are influenced by the fact that the American is
a black from a working-class background. His docu-
ments show that he neither drinks nor smokes and
that he sends all his money home.

174. Presley, John. "The Soldier." Kansas Quarterly,
        2, 1 (Winter 1969-70), 86-101.

Slatermore, a career Army sergeant, is a patient in
a military hospital in the United States. After learning that his former unit in Vietnam had been badly
mauled in an ambush, he got drunk and crashed a car,
killing two women and injuring himself. As he under-

goes treatment, he remembers scenes from his military career, including Vietnam.

175.   Richie, Mary. "Hunt and Destroy." New American
        Review, 6, (1969), 64-68. Also in Gulassa,
        Cyril M. (ed.). The Fact of Fiction. San
        Francisco: Canfield Press, 1972. 75-184742.
        pp. 99-103.

Jimmy is an enlisted member of a Marine reconnaissance unit in a war among the rice paddies of what
seems to be Vietnam. On one operation, he acquires
a pet snake. On another, a cobra comes between him
and an enemy soldier. Jimmy identifies with snakes.
He is an able and unfeeling being in a war situation
that is much more symbolic than realistic.

176.   Steiber, Raymond. "The Lost Indemnity." Trace,
        53 (1964), 166-172.

In a war that must be Vietnam, a lieutenant and an enlisted man are on patrol at night. The enlisted man is
terrified of the enemy and of the dark. He loses his
weapon, makes unnecessary noise, and plans to stop
the lieutenant from killing an enemy soldier. As they
return to their own lines, the enlisted man makes his
way successfully through the perimeter barbed wire,
but the lieutenant is trapped. The enlisted man leaves
him there to die.

177.   Suddick, Tom. "On Making the Same Mistake Twice."
        Samisdat, 26, 2 (1980), 18-23.

A Marine squad returning from a medical visit to a
village near the Demilitarized Zone comes under mortar fire from both friendly and unfriendly forces. It
develops that part of the problem is reliance on an
old French map. One of the men in the squad reflects
on similarities between the French and American oc-
cupations of Vietnam.

POETRY

178. Baker, Richard E. Shell Burst Pond. Tacoma,
        Washington: The Rapier Press, 1980. 26pp.

        Baker served as an infantryman in Vietnam. Some
        of the poems describe his experiences there and his
        impressions in grisly detail. Others touch on philo-
        sophical and romantic topics.

179. Balaban, John. After Our War. Pittsburgh: Univer-
        sity of Pittsburgh Press, 1974. 84pp. 73-13313.

        Balaban appears to be a particularly sensitive and
        able poet. Many of the poems and prose pieces in
        this collection relate to Vietnam, although not always
        to military matters there.

180. Balaban, John. Vietnam Poems. Oxford: Carcanet
        Press, 1970. 16pp.

        Several of these six poems are set in Vietnam. Pre-
        fatory material states that six hundred copies of this
        work were published.

181. Barry, Jan, and W. D. Ehrhart (eds.). Demilitarized
        Zones. Perkasie, Pennsylvania: East River
        Anthology, 1976. 182pp. 76-17200.

        The subtitle is "Veterans After Vietnam," but many
        of these poems are directly about the war. The edi-
        tors are both qualified and well placed to do their
        job, and they make a fine selection of the work of

many poets. This is an important anthology of Vietnam war poetry.

182. Berkhoudt, John C. Vietnam: A Year Before the
      "Peace." New York: Carlton Press, Inc.,
      1975. 48pp.

      Berkhoudt served in Vietnam as an infantry officer.
      His poems are of various lengths and styles.

183. Berry, D. C. saigon cemetery. Athens: University
      of Georgia Press, 1972. 50pp. 78-169949.

      The brief, spare poems in this collection are untitled,
      but they are clearly separate, rather than chapters
      of a single long poem. The jacket indicates that Berry
      was a medical officer in Vietnam.

184. Bly, Robert, and David Ray (eds.). A Poetry Reading
      Against the Vietnam War. Madison, Minnesota:
      The Sixties Press, 1966. 63pp. 66-4861.

      It is not always the case that collections of protest or
      antiwar poetry include anything actually set in Vietnam.
      In this instance, among the work of such persons as
      Adolf Hitler, I. F. Stone, and Walt Whitman, there
      are a number of Vietnam poems as well.

185. Casey, Michael. Obscenities. New Haven: Yale
      University Press, 1972. 68pp. 78-179470.

      The poems combine to form a sort of narration of
      Casey's experience as a rear-area military policeman
      in Vietnam. Thoughtful definitions of obscure military
      terms and slang are provided at the bottom of various
      pages.

186. Clover, Timothy. The Leaves of My Trees, Still
      Green. Chicago: Adams Press, 1970. 99pp.

      Clover was killed in Vietnam in 1968. Many of the

poems here were written long before his military
service, but more recent ones relate to Vietnam and
to the Army. The copy in hand was reproduced from
a typescript with corrections entered in pen and pen-
cil.

187.   Connell, Robert.   Firewinds; Poems on the Vietnam
            War.   Sydney: The Wentworth Press, 1968.
            21pp.   68-141365.

        There are eight poems, ranging in length from a few
        lines to two pages.   Also included are eight black-and-
        white drawings.   The illustrators are identified as
        David Ogg and Chris Amitzboll.

188.   Eastlake, William.   A Child's Garden of Verses for
            the Revolution.   New York: Grove Press, Inc.,
            1970.   240pp.   72-121419.

        About a third of the poems and brief prose pieces in
        this collection relate to Vietnam, where Eastlake vis-
        ited as a journalist.   The poems touch on a number
        of subjects related to the war, including racial mat-
        ters, American values in the war, and the prospect of
        death.   The prose pieces appear to be nonfiction ac-
        counts of Eastlake's experiences in Vietnam.

189.   Ehrhart, W. D.   The Awkward Silence.   Stafford,
            Virginia: Northwoods Press, Inc., 1980.   41pp.
            79-92943.

        As a poet and editor, Bill Ehrhart is clearly one of
        the major figures in Vietnam War literature.   He
        served as a sergeant in the Marines in Vietnam in
        1967 and 1968, often as a scout in combat.   This
        collection includes poems that appear in earlier works.

190.   Ehrhart, W. D.   A Generation of Peace.   New York:
            New Voices Publishing Company, 1975.   49pp.
            74-18995.

        The dust wrapper explains that this work was done

as an undergraduate thesis at Swarthmore College.
The poems, however, seem mature and capable. Well
over half of them relate to the poet's experience in the
Vietnam War.

191.   Ehrhart, W. D. A Generation of Peace. Samisdat,
        14, 3, 54th release, 1977. 32pp.

        This is a limited selection of the poems printed in
        Ehrhart's earlier work of the same title. There are
        also a few new poems here. Ehrhart's work fills this
        whole issue of the periodical, Samisdat.

192.   Ehrhart, W. D.   The Samisdat Poems of W. D. Ehr-
        hart. Samisdat, 24, 1, 93rd release, 1980.
        72pp.

        In this collection are many poems, sometimes revised,
        that appear in other works Ehrhart has written and
        edited. The typeface, legibility, and other physical
        qualities of this work are much superior to earlier
        Samisdat publications. Most of the poems here emerge
        from Ehrhart's experiences as a Marine sergeant in
        Vietnam.

193.   Floyd, Bryan Alec. The Long War Dead. New York:
        Avon Books, 1976. 95pp. 75-27440.

        Each poem is titled with the rank and name of a Ma-
        rine, and serves as his description or, in some cases,
        his epitaph. Descriptions of the circumstances of
        death in combat are both graphic and wry. There is
        a continuity to this book that is lacking in much Viet-
        nam War poetry.

194.   Gray, Nigel. Aftermath. Lancaster, England: Lan-
        caster University Students' Union, nd. 24pp.

        The seventeen poems here all relate in some way to
        the Vietnam War. They seem rather less descriptive
        than most poems by Americans. The book includes
        several black-and-white drawings by Vo-Kinh.

195. Gray, Nigel (ed.). Phoenix Country. Fireweed, 6
     (September 1976). 188pp.

     This special issue of the English literary journal
     Fireweed is dedicated to the British Hospital in Viet-
     nam, and everything in it has something to do with
     that country or with the war. There are black-and-
     white photographs, many poems, songs, and both fic-
     tion and nonfiction prose pieces. Notable is the in-
     clusion of some work by Vietnamese authors.

196. Hollis, Jocelyn. Vietnam Poems; The War Poems of
     Today. New York: American Poetry Press,
     1979. 38pp.

     All of the poems are about the war, and some are
     set in Vietnam. The images and narration are not
     particularly realistic. A biographical note about the
     author says nothing about any firsthand experience in
     Vietnam.

197. Johnson, G. P. I Was Fighting for Peace, but, Lord,
     There Was Much More. Hicksville, New York:
     Exposition Press, 1979. 88pp.

     Johnson served as an infantryman in Vietnam in 1968
     and 1969. The first section of poems relates to that
     experience, describing his reaction to a new country
     and, for example, to his first act of killing. The
     poet's strong Christian faith is apparent in his work.

198. Kiley, Fred, and Tony Dater (eds.). Listen, the War.
     Colorado Springs: The Air Force Academy As-
     sociation of Graduates, 1973. 157pp.

     This is certainly the most important book of Air
     Force poetry to emerge from the Vietnam War. The
     editors, assigned to the U. S. Air Force Academy,
     sought poems from many sources and originally consid-
     ered three thousand from which the contents of this
     book were selected. Most, but not all, of the poems
     relate to Air Force subjects.

199.   Kilmer, Forest L. (comp. and ed.). Boondock
       Bards. San Francisco: Pacific Stars and Stripes,
       1968. 122pp.

       Virtually all the poets here were American servicemen
       in Vietnam who sent their poems to the Pacific Stars
       and Stripes in the mid-1960s. They are not all good
       poets, but their honesty and sincerity are unmistakable.
       Location or unit designation is given for all.

200.   Layne, McAvoy. How Audie Murphy Died in Vietnam.
       Garden City, New York: Anchor Books, 1973.
       120pp. approximately. 72-96279.

       The lack of page numbers, a table of contents, or an
       index of any kind makes this book rather awkward.
       The poems all seem to deal with Vietnam and the war
       as they take Murphy into Marine boot camp and through
       various combat and rear-area experiences. Most of
       the poems occupy less than one page, and many are
       much shorter than that.

201.   Lowenfels, Walter (ed.). Where Is Vietnam? Garden
       City, New York: Anchor Books, 1967. 160pp.

       Among the eighty-seven poets represented in this an-
       thology are James Dickey, Hayden Carruth, Lawrence
       Ferlinghetti, and Denise Levertov. Most are new
       poems, and some were written for various anti-Vietnam
       readings in the 1960s.

202.   McCarthy, Gerald. War Story. Trumansburg, New
       York: The Crossing Press, 1977. 69pp. 77-
       23320.

       The poet was a Marine in Vietnam. Many of the
       poems in the first half of the book describe his ex-
       periences and impressions there and upon his return
       to the United States.

203.   McDonald, Walter. Caliban in Blue and Other Poems.
       Lubbock: Texas Tech Press, 1976. 51pp.

The title poem is divided into a number of shorter
poems that all seem to emerge from the experiences
of a fighter pilot in Vietnam. The subjects vary from
tiger attacks to post exchanges to hospitals. McDonald is a capable poet.

204.   Martin, Earl E. A Poet Goes to War. Bozeman,
          Montana: Big Sky Books, 1970. 78pp.

The untitled poems are grouped in several headings
and reflect Martin's military training, service in
Korea, service in Vietnam during the 1968 Tet Offensive, and homecoming. The information "About
the Poet" reveals that Martin was wounded while serving in an Army armored unit.

205.   Oldham, Perry. Vinh Long. Meadows of Dan, Vir-
          ginia: Northwoods Press, Inc., 1976. 56pp.

These brief poems deal with many aspects of a soldier's life in Vietnam. Their format and style vary
widely. The copy in hand is unfortunately rather
badly made, with margins that in some cases cut into
the text and with uneven inking throughout.

206.   Rottmann, Larry, Jan Barry, and Basil T. Paquet
          (eds.). Winning Hearts and Minds. Brooklyn,
          New York: 1st Casualty Press, 1972. 119pp.

The publisher is a company formed of members of the
Vietnam Veterans Against the War, and that organization also assisted in collecting the works of the thirty-
three poets represented. The works are arranged to
reflect a sort of tour in Vietnam. An index provides
the poets' former military rank and unit as well as
any decorations awarded to each one.

207.   Scott, L. E. Time Came Hunting Time. Cammeray,
          Australia: Saturday Centre Books, 1978. 56pp.

According to preliminary material, Scott is a black
American who lives in New Zealand. His text includes

poems, brief prose pieces, and short stories. The
poems and miscellaneous prose are all brief--usually
less than a page. The short stories are described
below.

207a.   "Three Hearts." pp. 38-50.

A black Army sergeant, Don Evans, is assisted
by other black enlisted men to arrange a transfer
to a rear area after receiving three Purple Hearts.
There is considerable emphasis on race relationships.

207b.   "Vietnam--April 4, 1968." pp. 51-55.

Williams, a black Army sergeant who is recovering from wounds in a hospital, is visited by several
friends. He learns that he is going home and that
Martin Luther King has been killed.

208.   Shea, Dick. Vietnam Simply. Coronado, California:
        The Pro Tem Publishers, 1967. 150pp. approx-
        imately.

Shea was a Navy lieutenant involved in underwater
operations in Vietnam, and the poems here reflect
his tour. They are untitled, and the book is unpaged.
At the rear is a list of what may be the titles of the
poems "in order of appearance." This arrangement
is quite awkward.

209.   Topham, J. (ed.). Poems of the Vietnam War. New
        York: American Poetry Press, 1980. 48pp.
        80-65621.

Although Topham is clearly listed as editor, rather
than the single poet, there is no indication that anyone
else had a part in this work. The poems vary greatly
in style, setting, length, and format, but no poets'
names are given. There is, however, an index of
first lines.

MISCELLANEOUS WORKS

210. Adair, Dick. Dick Adair's Saigon. New York:
          Weatherhill, 1971. 144pp. 78-157268.

The focus of this large and well-printed book is almost entirely upon the city of Saigon. Most of the
subjects of Adair's black-and-white drawings are people. Settings include the city streets, commercial
enterprises, the port, and military backgrounds.

211. Aument, Shary. Unforgettable Faces. Kalamazoo,
          Michigan: Leaders Press, 1972. 216pp.

In 1971 and 1972, Aument, a private individual, worked
through POW and MIA organizations to obtain photographs of American prisoners and men missing in action in Vietnam. The drawings based on those photographs are all black-and-white, full-face, head-and-
shoulder poses. Each drawing is accompanied by a
letter from a member of the man's family. Many are
quite touching.

212. Heroes and Heroines of South Vietnam. Peking: Sup-
          plement to China Reconstructs, July 1965. 19pp.

The sixteen plates in this loose portfolio are in various media, including paintings, drawings, and wood-
block prints. Accompanied by brief captions, they
show scenes of heroic peasants and workers defeating
imperialist American aggressors or their South Vietnamese puppet soldiers.

213. Hodgson, Michael T. With Sgt. Mike in Vietnam.

Washington, D. C.: Army Times Publishing
Company, 1970. 119pp.

Hodgson is the "Sgt. Mike" of the title. He served
with the Marines in Vietnam, and the several continuing characters in these often humorous cartoons are
also Marines. Many of the cartoons are reprinted
from civilian and military periodicals.

214. Lee, Ron (ed.). Absolutely No U.S. Personnel Per-
      mitted Beyond This Point. New York: Delta,
      1972. 100pp. approximately.

This collection of cartoons is introduced by Jules
Feiffer, and the editor is identified as a member of
the National Peace Action Coalition. Sources of the
cartoons are newspapers and journals worldwide.
Most are critical of the U.S. role in Vietnam; others
express anti-American themes more generally.

215. Melvin, Ken. Sorry 'Bout That! Tokyo: The Way-
      ward Press, 1966. 103pp.

The book jacket explains that Ken Melvin is a name
chosen by two persons, both with extensive experience
in Vietnam. They combine black-and-white cartoons
with jokes, captioned photographs, verse, and other
elements thought to be humorous. Most of the drawings are the work of a single artist.

216. Melvin, Ken. "Be Nice." Tokyo: The Wayward
      Press, 1966. 100pp.

In this sequel to their earlier Sorry 'Bout That, the
two persons who write as Ken Melvin present another,
very similar, collection of Vietnam cartoons, jokes,
verse, clippings, and short prose pieces.

217. "Super Realistic War Comics." np, nd, 4pp.

There is no publication information in the usual sense,
but one of the panels in this single-fold, black-and-

white comic urges readers to call the Draft Action
Group--Resistance, in New Haven (Connecticut?).
Among the cartoonists whose work appears are R.
Crumb, R. Cobb, and Jules Feiffer.

218. Tauber, Burton R. "Preliminary Prospectus: The
       War in Vietnam. " New York: Workman Pub-
       lishing Company, Inc., 1970. 16pp.

This is one of the most subtle and sophisticated pieces
of Vietnam War humor. With a light touch, Tauber
offers a high-risk investment with such dangers as
pacification, Cambodian operations, and aggressive
competition. Everything is in the form of a typical
common stock prospectus.

219. Trudeau, G. B. Bravo for Life's Little Ironies.
       New York: Popular Library, 1971. 80pp. ap-
       proximately. 72-91561.

This is a selection of cartoons from Trudeau's But
This War Had Such Promise. Most of the cartoons
selected reflect the war, rather than the other subjects in the larger work.

220. Trudeau, G. B. But This War Had Such Promise.
       New York: Holt, Rinehart and Winston, 1971.
       100pp. approximately. 72-91561.

The "Doonesbury" cartoon series is well known to
many Americans, and the cartoonist's political and
social ideas are as clear as his great talent. The
principal characters in this collection are B.D., the
gung-ho former football player, and Phred, the Vietcong terrorist. Their relationship is developed in
numerous delightful, almost classic, panels. Cartoons on Kent State, ecology, race relations, politics,
and other subjects from the period of the war complete the collection.

221. Tuso, Joseph F. (ed.). Folksongs of the American
       Fighter Pilot in Southeast Asia, 1967-1968.

Folklore Forum, Bibliographic and Special Series, #7, 1971. 28pp.

Tuso provides a responsible and scholarly introduction
as well as a useful glossary. The mimeographed
typescript is a modest format for this important collection of lyrics to pilots' songs. Notes for most
songs indicate the tune to which they are sung.

222.   Verdicts on Vietnam. London: Pemberton Publishing
            Co., 1968. 128pp.

Edited by "ABU" and introduced by James Cameron,
this international collection of antiwar and anti-
American cartoons is divided into several sections
that reflect the beginning and growth of American
participation in the Vietnam War.

223.   Vietnam Combat Art. New York: Cavanagh & Cav-
            anagh, 1968. 86pp.

This selection from the Marine Corps Combat Art
Collection is introduced by H. Lester Cooke of the
National Gallery. The works are in various media
and styles. Most are black-and-white. The book's
large format and excellent physical qualities enhance
reproduction. The explanatory captions by Raymond
Henri are accurate, substantial, and informative.
The work naturally emphasizes the U.S. Marine Corps
in Vietnam.

224.   Waterhouse, Charles. Vietnam Sketchbook. Rutland,
            Vermont: Charles E. Tuttle Company, 1968.
            127pp. 68-21114.

Many of the black-and-white sketches are set in the
area of the Mekong Delta. Waterhouse visited there
in 1967, and his work reveals his obvious affection
for the American servicemen who are most often his
subjects.

225.   Waterhouse, Charles. Vietnam War Sketches. Rut-

land, Vermont: Charles E. Tuttle Company,
1970. 127pp. 71-119410.

The work here is similar to Waterhouse's earlier
Vietnam Sketches. Realistic and engaging black-and-
white drawings have captions of one or two sentences.
Waterhouse renders military subjects with effective accuracy.

226. West, Richard. Sketches from Vietnam. London:
Jonathan Cape, 1968 (© 1966). 159pp.

The text is an account of the author's travels through
Vietnam in the 1960s. The twenty black-and-white
illustrations by Gerald Scarfe are mostly caricatures
of Vietnamese and Americans.

DRAMA

227. Balk, H. Wesley. The Dramatization of 365 Days.
Minneapolis: University of Minnesota Press,
1972. 148pp. 72-85756.

This play is based on 365 Days, by Ronald J. Glasser
(Braziller, 1971), a nonfiction account of an Army
doctor at a hospital in Japan. In the introduction,
Balk explains how the original work was adapted for
chamber theater. The characters are Speaker 1,
Speaker 2, etc., and they describe and portray events
both in the hospital and in Vietnam. Accounts of
combat and of wounds are especially graphic and brutal. Passionless medical language is used to convey
the harm done to men's bodies by weapons of war.
Balk includes photographs from a production of the
play, ground plans, and a helpful glossary.

228. Gray, Amlin. How I Got That Story. New York:
Dramatists Play Service, Inc., 1981 (© 1979).
64pp.

In a telephone conversation with the compiler, Gray
described his notional country of "Am-bo Land" as an
analog to Vietnam. The two characters include a
wire-service Reporter, and the Historical Event, an
individual who portrays various government officials,
Americans, Vietnamese civilians, Vietcong, and other
parties to the war. When the Reporter arrives in
Am-bo Land directly from East Dubuque, he is bewildered by a place plagued with war, suffering, and
death, but without honesty or truth. After numerous
adventures, the Reporter sinks into the culture of
Am-bo Land; he loses his journalistic objectivity and

103

purpose and becomes instead part of the story. At
the end, an American photographer takes his picture
as an illustration of the locale.

229.   Kustow, Michael, and others (eds.). The Book of
        US. London: Calder and Boyars, 1968. 214pp.
        Indianapolis: The Bobbs-Merrill Company, 1968.

The text of the play US amounts to about half of this
publication. The remainder includes an exhaustive
account of the background, production, and critical
reaction to the play. The strong and articulate feelings of everyone involved with the play about the Vietnam War are stated often. The play itself is in two
acts; the first seeks to depict American involvement
in the war; the second appears to be focused on reaction to the war in England. The book is laid out
so that the script is mixed with lengthy footnotes,
songs, cartoons, photographs, and other peripheral
items in a manner that leads to some confusion.
American characters are stupid, brutal, and venal,
while the Vietnamese are heroic patriots. It is interesting to see such a virulent anti-American theme
in an English play.

230.   Rabe, David. The Basic Training of Pavlo Hummel
        and Sticks and Bones. New York: The Viking
        Press, 1973 (© 1969). 72-75746. 228pp.

A substantial introduction explains something of the
creative background and production history of both
works and includes a cogent statement of Rabe's opinion of "antiwar" drama. "The Basic Training of Pavlo
Hummel" begins with Hummel's death from a terrorist's grenade in Vietnam. Pavlo then finds himself
back in Army basic training. This, and indeed the
rest of the play, may occur in the dying Pavlo's mind.
After experiences with both cadre and other trainees
that are typical for an Army recruit, Pavlo Hummel
returns to Vietnam in the second act. He serves as
medic until he is killed again by another grenade,
thrown this time by an American. Throughout the
play, Pavlo's innocence is gradually replaced by toughness in a sensitive revelation of the effect of war on

men. In "Sticks and Bones," David, a veteran blinded
in the war, is delivered by truck to the home of his
parents, Ozzie and Harriet, and his brother, Ricky.
David and the specter of his Vietnamese girlfriend,
Zung, destroy the complacent and ordinary life of
the household and particularly upset and challenge
Ozzie. In the end, his parents and his brother help
David to slash his wrists.

231.   Reich, David. The War That Never Ends. White-
           water, Wisconsin: typescript, 1980. 22pp.

For Dusty, a Vietnam veteran with a missing leg,
the war is still very much a part of life some twelve
years after his discharge. The amputation affects his
job, his attitude, and his marriage. Also, he is
haunted by explicit dreams of Vietnam in which persons he has killed return to speak to him. In conversations among Dusty and other Vietnam veterans,
the idea emerges that they are much less understood
and appreciated by society than were the veterans of
earlier wars. However, Dusty's growing relationship
with a patriotic World War II veteran ends the play on
an optimistic note. The five characters and straight-
forward action suggest that this would be a good play
for a small company, although the going is a bit heavy
when the characters quote statistics about Vietnam to
one another.

232.   Ribman, Ronald. The Final War of Ollie Winter.
           New York: CBS Television Network, 1967.
           91pp.

This finely printed script includes still photographs
from the 1967 CBS television production. The play
is set in the jungle of Vietnam in 1963. Ollie Winter is a black U.S. Army master sergeant who is the
sole survivor of a Vietnamese patrol he advised. As
Winter runs from the pursuing Vietcong, he picks up
a Vietnamese girl, a baby, and a prisoner along the
way. Flashbacks relate to Winter's harsh youth in
the United States and help establish his empathy with
the poor people of Vietnam. After a stop in a village,
Winter and the girl are finally caught and killed by

the Vietcong. This play offers a notably sympathetic
view of the American effort in Vietnam.

233.   Terry, Megan. Viet Rock. New York: Simon and
          Schuster, 1967. 67-17889. 282pp.

This parody of the Vietnam experience emphasizes
action rather than individuals. Scenes in the United
States and in Vietnam feature soldiers' parents, U.S.
senators, and the Madonna. Continuing characters
are a Sergeant, who mouths simpleminded pro-Amer-
ican and pro-military slogans, and a group of his men
who seem to represent all American soldiers. The
Sergeant trains his men and leads them into combat
in Vietnam, where they suffer both wounds and death.
North Vietnamese characters, including the broad-
caster Hanoi Hannah, appear to speak lines represent-
ing their points of view about the war. In an alterna-
tive final scene, presented at the end of the ordinary
script, Americans are captured, tortured, and murdered by North Vietnamese. In a performance, all
of this action would probably convey an appropriate
sense of diversity and confusion about the war.

APPENDIX: WORKS NOT SEEN

Novels

234. Elliot, Ellen. Vietnam Nurse. Arcadia House, 1969.

235. Front Lines: Soldiers' Writings from Vietnam. Indochina Curriculum Group, 1975.

236. Proud, Franklin M., and Alfred F. Eberhardt. Tiger in the Mountains. New York: St. Martin's Press, 1976.

237. Ross, William. Bamboo Terror. Rutland, Vermont: Citadel Press, 1970.

238. Tam, H. T. Saigon 7. Saigon: A Damson Book, 1968.

239. Vu, Nguyen. Back from Hell. Saigon: Dia Nga, 1969.

240. Werder, Albert D. A Spartan Education. Brooklyn, New York: Beekman Publishers, 1978.

Poetry

241. Alley, Rewi. The Mistake: Poems. Christchurch, New Zealand: Caxton Press, 1965.

242. Guilmar, Cesar. Saigon, via U.P.I. np: np, 1969.

243. We Promise One Another; Poems from the Asian War.

Washington, D. C.:   Indochina Mobile Education
Project, 1971.

Miscellaneous

244.   Stewart, George.   What's So Funny About Vietnam?
Tampa, Florida: Tampa Art & Pub. Co., 1968.

AUTHOR INDEX